of
Water

athleen Jamie is an internationally regarded poet and
ssayist. Her writing is rooted in Scottish landscape and culture,
shown in her acclaimed essay collections *Findings*,
ghtlines and *Surfacing*. Her award-winning poetry collections
lude *The Tree House* and *The Bonniest Companie*. In 2018,
nie was elected as a Fellow of the Royal Society of Edinburgh.
e lives in Scotland.

KathleenJamie | kathleenjamie.com

'A selection of luminous essays, poems and visual art . . . The
most intuitive pieces reflect that nature is not something to
be explored on weekends and in nice weather but through
everyday rituals . . . [written with] a gallows humour and
deftness of touch'
The Times

'Beautiful . . . A series of authentic experiences, each
individual immersing themselves in nature . . . *Antlers of Water*
is a warm invitation to reimagine your intimacy to nature,
whether that's within the confinements of a communal city
garden or on an island surrounded by the vast ocean'
Caught by the River, Book of the Month

Antlers
of
Water

Writing on the Nature and
Environment of Scotland

Edited by

KATHLEEN JAMIE

CANONGATE

This paperback edition published in 2021 by Canongate Books

First published in Great Britain, the USA and Canada in 2020
by Canongate Books Ltd, 14 High Street, Edinburgh EH1 1TE

Distributed in the USA by Publishers Group West
and in Canada by Publishers Group Canada

canongate.co.uk

1

British Library Cataloguing-in-Publication Data
A catalogue record for this book is available on
request from the British Library

ISBN 978 1 78689 981 1

The publisher acknowledges support from the
National Lottery through Creative Scotland
towards the publication of this title

Typeset in Bembo Std by
Palimpsest Book Production Ltd, Falkirk, Stirlingshire

Printed and bound in Great Britain by Clays Ltd, Elcograf S.p.A.

Contents

Introduction

KATHLEEN JAMIE

*A*ntlers of Water is a collection of specially commissioned writing which concerns our relationship with the more-than-human world. It announces a 'new Scottish nature writing' and brings together, for the first time, a fine selection of our country's hugely talented contemporary nature and environmental writers. It features prose and poetry which is by turns personal, celebratory, political, frightened and hopeful. All the writers in this book are alive in this difficult moment; all reside, or have resided, in Scotland; and all are writing here about some aspect of the country they call home. Their work addresses the realities of our times, and examines our relationship with our fellow creatures, our beloved and fast-changing landscapes, our energy futures, our ancient past.

We talk about a 'new' Scottish nature writing, but of course Scottish nature writing is far from new. There is a long tradition: birds animate the ancient ballads, often bringing messages, as they do still. In 1785 Robert Burns famously addressed the mouse whose nest he'd accidentally destroyed, and Duncan Ban MacIntyre's hymn to Ben Dorain and its deer was also composed in that century. Much-loved classics of nature writing have featured Scottish landscapes, like Gavin Maxwell's *Ring of Bright Water* and Nan Shepherd's (vastly different) *The Living Mountain*. Our own title *Antlers of Water* is taken from Norman MacCaig's mid-twentieth-century poem 'Looking Down on Glen Canisp'. We have always shown kind attention to our land and its non-human creatures; we have sung and painted and photographed our extraordinarily beautiful country. But what is different about the twenty-first century, what makes our nature writing 'new', is our increasing awareness of unfolding ecological crisis.

The idea lingers of Scotland as a place of lochs and bens and faraway islands, a wild and romantic place where one may forget our human travails. Even if that was once true, it is not now. There can be no one who has not heard of climate change, which we now see rapidly changing the world around us; no one unaware of the mounting levels of threat facing wildlife through habitat loss and want of food; no one can be unaware of ocean plastic and chemical pollution. Our writers are fully cognisant of environmental crisis, they don't pretend it's not happening, but they are not prophets of doom. Twenty-one writers and two visual artists were asked to contribute to this book; all responded at once, with great enthusiasm. All responded, I believe, out of love of the world, and our particular part of it. They are not offering escapism. They know it is not possible nowadays to 'escape' into nature, and find temporary relief from some other 'real' world – far from it. The natural world, the world which birthed us and sustains us, is where the biggest and most frightening changes are happening. What the writers in this volume are doing, in their very different ways, is meeting the challenge of finding a way of speaking and writing, witnessing and celebrating as they continue to love the world, its landforms and plants and creatures, even as we navigate a crisis. The natural world is not here as a painted backdrop to our human concern: it *is* our human concern.

So our writers are aware of global issues, but also, whether they like it or not, they are familiar with Scotland's peculiarities: its tourist appeal and lingering Romanticisation; its ongoing tension between economic exploitation and conservation; its chronic issues around land ownership and dispossession; its restive political situation; its vast, beautiful coastline; its infamous weather. Some of the writers within are capable of great physical feats of walking and endurance; others live lives more circumscribed. We have writing from the mothers of newborns and toddlers, mothers railing against the inequality their daughters are still subjected to. We have fathers alarmed by the damage nuclear waste is laying down in the environment, into their children's future. Indeed, the range of concerns is as various as Scotland itself, from uninhabited island to tenement block, from rockpool to eagle's flight, from red deer to pigeons. We present traditional prose through song to experimental poetry, but what all the writers share is an *attentiveness*. They have chosen to foreground the natural world, in some way, in their work. As Hugh MacDiarmid said, 'Scotland, small?'

Recent years have seen a renaissance of so-called 'nature writing' throughout the English-speaking world. There are shelves in bookshops where before there were none, literary prizes, specialist journals. Many of the books which fill those 'Nature and Environment' shelves are made in Scotland, and individual Scottish writers have been at the forefront of that wider movement, but, we ask, is there an identifiably *Scottish* new nature writing? Writers from all over the country were invited to contribute to this book. Not all were born here, many have chosen to live here, or found themselves obliged to. Some are well established as writers, having held their own as nature writers before its recent celebration. Others are just beginning. Their work arrived from Shetland, Sutherland, Perthshire, the Inner Hebrides, an Edinburgh tenement, the fields of Angus, the semi-militarised Firth of Forth, the woods of Galloway. But is there an identifiably S*cottish* streak to their work?

There's certainly a language. Readers might discover some Scots words they did not know before, but if there is a Scottish *attitude* to our own country, well, that is for readers to decide. I would only point out that in this book, the words 'wild' and 'wilderness' rarely occur. It's not our daily lived experience of our own land. What the writers observe is the intersection of modernity and nature in a rapidly changing Scotland. Wind turbines, housing schemes, wee back gardens – such is the Scottish environment we know. Many of the writers live in urban settings: most Scots do. We have been largely removed from the land and, despite a few community buy-outs, our experience of our own land and nature is not one of ownership, certainly not of the landscapes that feature on calendars. It's only in recent years that our right to roam or wild-camp has been established, but, as this book shows, you don't have to wild-camp to be an eco-poet. We have space, but the 'wild' is actually hard to find. Human intervention is everywhere. Yes, there are sea-eagles, but their re-introduction is the result of human political and conservation activity (as the absence of raptors is so often the result of human greed and cruelty). There are expansive peat-moors; there are also wind farms. There are rugged Atlantic shorelines, but they are littered with plastic trash. The writers in this book do not pretend Scotland is pristine; rather, they engage knowledgeably with its culture and history, and, crucially, its future. Ancient life-ways are acknowledged, lingering in place-names and archaeological sites, but certain so-called 'traditions' are briskly challenged. There is eco-anxiety, 'solastalgia', feminism; there are the ruins of capitalist endeavour. There is also plenty of space (habitat?) for our fellow creatures, from stags to barnacles, which share our 'Scotland small' and of whom we can be so negligent.

*

All is not yet lost. In Scotland we are experiencing species decline and habitat loss, but we do still have astonishing landscapes, the ocean is never far away, and some vital rewilding and conservation projects are afoot, with more being mooted all the time. Very many of us support one conservation body or another. Forty years ago, there were no sea-eagles or beavers in Scotland. Now there are. Ospreys are back. But the thrilling, raucous sea-bird colonies are declining. We are trying to wean ourselves off oil in favour of wind and tidal energy, with promising results. The effect of turbines on our land and seascapes is explored within this book. As we realise we must halt destruction, reduce emissions and renegotiate our relationship with the natural world, our *noticing* is a vital contribution. Out of our noticing comes our art and our writing. For me, this noticing and caring, this attention, this writing from within personal circumstances, whether about an insect or a mountain, amounts to a political act. In a time of ecological crisis, I would argue that simply insisting on our right to pay heed to natural landscapes and other non-human lifeforms amounts to an act of resistance to the forces of destruction. It doesn't actually take much to be an eco-writer or a nature poet. It begins when you pay attention to the world, and to language, and strive to bring the two together. This writing matters. And so, crucially, does our reading.

Here is *Antlers of Water*. There are in Scotland more writers and activists than are published here. A new generation of Scottish writers is already emerging who will soon be making waves of their own. Stags, wasps, eagles and barnacles await you. Islands and rivers. Windowsills. We invite you to read not as a passive recipient, but as an active participant in this vital work, this noticing. If by reading you are encouraged or confirmed in your love of the natural world, if your interest is piqued, if you're inspired simply to put the book down and look outside, then our job is done. When we read and write, when we love our fellow creatures, when we walk on the beach, when we just listen and notice, we are not little cogs in the machine, but part of the remedy.

Getting the Hang of the Wind

CHRIS POWICI

I lean my bike against Turbine 20 and listen. The sound of turbine blades spinning in the wind is tough to describe. It's such a strange noise, neither wholly natural nor wholly mechanical, that the best I can manage is *heavy whump*. W.B. Yeats' description of the swans at Coole Park comes to mind: 'the bell-beat of their wings above my head'. 'Bell-beat' feels about right – a sonorous, rhythmic mixing of the human and the wild.

I gaze up at the blades. This is no cute and homely windmill from a children's picture book. This is the modern world at work – vast, gleaming scythes, cutting the air – and the thought strikes that comparing them to swans' wings may be some kind of aesthetic blasphemy, a diabolical confusion of the industrial with the natural.

These are the Braes of Doune, an area of rough, hill-ocky upland moor which lies across the Highland Fault Line about twelve miles north of Stirling – the very heart of Scotland, if the tourist brochures are to be believed. These hills don't possess the raw glamour of the high mountains of the Cairngorms or the deeply forested peaks of the Trossachs. The Braes of Doune never have been much of a draw for the passionate hillwalker. But some folk reckon their more modest beauty is just fine. Or it was, at least, until the wind farm came. After the last of the thirty-six turbines had been erected in 2006, a correspondent to the *Herald* wrote, 'it can only be assumed that those who live in the Stirling area had no idea previously just what visual obscenities wind farms are. Well, they ken noo.'

The correspondent will have his supporters. There are plenty who've denounced wind farms as a hideous blemish on the land and an assault on our sensibilities. The trouble is, I ken no such thing. I was cycling a flat, low road in the Carse of Stirling when I caught sight of the first of the turbines being erected, high on the hills to the north. They were tall and fiercely, brilliantly white, standing in vivid contrast to the muted greens and browns of the moor. But they didn't seem ugly or obscene; they didn't look beautiful, either. They looked, well, *strange*. The strangeness was beguiling at first: they seemed like monuments to a lost religion, or a religion still taking root.

To be standing, some fifteen years later, among the turbines is to realise the sheer scale of the enterprise. They cover a whole lot of moor, more or less a thousand acres, dominating the view for miles. But it's the height that that takes the breath. At about sixty metres a wind turbine is twice the height of Doune Castle, and the impression of some kind of quasi-religious purpose hasn't quite disappeared. A circle of boulders has been placed around the base of each turbine (presumably as ballast for the foundations). The echoes of Callanish or Stonehenge are unmistakable. But the echoes are faint. After all, a wind farm serves the very secular purpose of generating the power that drives our TVs, cookers, computers, washing machines and fridges. It helps keep the lights on in our streets. It's as much a part of industry as a coal mine or an oil rig.

After the knee-buckling slog of pedalling uphill for the best part of two hours I decide it's time to work my legs another way. I walk along the wind farm track towards the moorland ridge. Behind me, to the south-east, a pale half-moon is showing through the blue deeps of the early evening sky. Ahead of me the bright, unclouded sun hangs low over the peak of Uamh Bheag. Apart from the wind, the only sound is the soft crunch of my shoes on the loose stones of the track. The only movement is the quiver of grass and the relentless shadows of turbine blades sweeping across the moor. Up here, things feel peaceful *and* weird.

Then something stirs in the heather. A red deer hind is watching me walk towards her. I pause. For a few seconds we stand, utterly still, gazing at one another. I forget all about the vastness of the turbines and the noise of the blades.

The hind turns and bounds silently across the moor until she is lost in a haze of evening sunlight. The noise returns. The question remains: can I still call this a wild place?

I've come up here before to see deer, or rather to hear them. Last autumn I pedalled and pushed the bike up to the site of the topmost turbine, some 1,600 feet above sea level, laid it on the ground and trudged across the moor until I found myself looking across Glen Artney, one of the most southerly of all the Highland glens. I couldn't see any deer but the rough, throaty roars of rutting stags rumbled and echoed across the moor, a primeval wild chant that's been heard every autumn in this and other glens since the last ice age. I stood up to my knees in peat and heather, enthralled and, truth to tell, unnerved. The roar of a stag reminds us that the world wasn't put together with human beings in mind. But this was happening in the shadow of the 'visual obscenity' of a wind farm; the roaring of the stags was caught up in the echo of the turbine blades. Just how wild was this place?

Deer are not the only creatures to call this place home. On my way up to the wind farm late this afternoon, where the road to the farms on the Braes becomes little more than a track, I saw a bird hanging in the air. I stopped to get a better look. I could tell from the shape of the tail – more tuning fork than fan – that this was no buzzard. And then there was the colour of the wing feathers: a deep reddish brown, like a splash of rust. This was a red kite.

The bird guide on the bookshelves at home claims that red kites are larger than buzzards, but they don't look it. Buzzards are all bulk and brawn; red kites are slenderness and grace. This one seemed keen to prove the point, floating less than thirty feet above me, at home on the breeze. I've no idea if it regarded me as a threat, an intrusion, or just some harmless curiosity – it's hard to read the look in the eye of a bird – but the expression on its pale grey face seemed more serene than savage, possessed by a kind of poise, a slow deliberate intent, as if those small dark eyes were constantly, calmly going about the business of mapping and re-mapping its world.

It gave no cry but after a minute turned and glided away across a sheep field, so effortlessly, so downright skilfully, I could tell at once that this bird knew the ways of the wind – all its twists and gusts and eddies. It called to mind a surfer riding a wave, letting the power of nature do the work. Eventually it disappeared behind a knot of woodland and I recommenced my altogether slower, clumsier progress up the track.

The presence of red kites in these hills is a small but glowing triumph of conservation. Forty years ago there were about fifty breeding pairs in Wales. And that was it as far as mainland Britain was concerned. In the name of pest control and game management, the red kite was driven to extinction in England by 1871 and in Scotland by 1879. Then in the 1980s reintroduction programmes began in earnest across the UK, including the country-side around Doune. Between 1996 and 2001, 103 birds were released into these hills. They've even helped put

Doune on the tourist map. Some people come for the castle (the backdrop to *Monty Python and the Holy Grail*, as well as *Outlander*); some people come for the distillery at nearby Deanston; and some people come for the kites. For a few pounds you can watch them up close from a hide at Argaty Red Kites, located a mile or two north of the village.

There had been fears that the wind farm would spell the end of Doune's red kites, that they wouldn't know how to deal with the spinning blades, that the noise would confuse them and if they didn't fall mangled at the feet of the turbines, they'd abandon the Braes of Doune for a more welcoming habitat.

Those fears have faded. When their numbers were monitored, just one bird per year was found to have been killed from flying into a turbine. This rate of loss is vanishingly small, especially if you compare it with the numbers of red kites 'lost' (i.e. shot or poisoned) in areas where grouse shoots are big business. These days the local population is thriving, divided between roosts to the north and south of the Braes of Doune.

If red kites can get the hang of wind farms, why not other species? It's an intriguing question for conservationists and for those many, many thousands of us who get a kick out of knowing there are other, wilder creatures forging a life among our woods and moors. Wolves may, for the time being, still lie beyond the pale but you don't have to be some kind of wildlife freak to make a persuasive case for the reintroduction of wildcats and even lynx. There are plenty of deer and hare to be hunted in this nook of the land, plenty of heather, grass and rock where a hunter can lie in wait.

But up here, on the moor itself, the wind farm makes its presence felt. I can see deer and red kites, I can dream of wildcat and lynx, but there's no getting away from the echoey sweep of the turbine blades. Bird counts are all very well, but when push comes to shove, we want – maybe even *need* – our wild places to look the part.

These feelings run deep. They matter. I can read books about habitat loss and biodiversity, I can study temperature graphs and rainfall charts, but our ecological emergency isn't just a question of statistics. I need to ask the question: what does the land *feel* like?

We need wilderness – mountains, moors and forests where the industrial world, in all its guises, has been kept at bay. These places need to exist for themselves and for the animals and plants that live there. And we need them to exist so that people can, as the saying goes, get away from it all – where 'all' stands for the noise, throb and sheer relentless grind of the human carry-on, a grind that's driven, in part at least, by our demand for cheap energy.

I can't bring myself to hate the Braes of Doune wind farm. It doesn't feel like a remnant of 'pure' wilderness. But it doesn't feel like a factory or an oil refinery either. I can't ignore the sheer size of the turbines, nor the din of them cutting and flailing at the air, but if I keep my eyes open, I can see deer and hare and red kites. I can feel the wind in my face as well as hear it pouring through the turbine blades.

★

Lynn Bowser and her son Tom run Argaty Red Kites as part of the family farm. Committed bird watchers and casual visitors come to learn about the local wildlife and see red kites. Once a day, Lynn and Tom leave 'snacks' for the kites (they don't want them to become dependent) and folk can watch as many as fifty wild birds of prey swoop down to the feeding station, wings spread, intent on a few scraps of meat and bone.

Lynn and Tom like the kites. The birds eat carrion rather than kill lambs; they help bolster the farm's finances and they're a spectacular sight, gathering at the feeding station or just gliding above the pastures and woods. Tom is even writing a book about them. 'But this isn't a theme park,' Lynn insisted when I dropped by ahead of my latest bike trip up to the wind turbines. She's right, of course. It's still a farm. It's still a way of making a living. Compromises need to be made. An overlap between the wild and the human has to be negotiated and managed.

Maybe it's that sense of overlap which is key if we're to nourish a new sense of the wild. Of course, what's left of what we like to call wilderness needs protecting – from energy schemes and golf courses and mile after dreadful mile of identikit Sitka plantations. The feeling of 'losing yourself' in a wood, or up a mountain or on an empty stretch of beach thrills the soul and puts our myopic, tech-hungry modern sensibilities to the test. But I don't want my experience of 'the wild' confined to nature reserves and protected habitats. I don't want a 'theme park' wilderness. I want the wild to be part of everyday life. I want to see buzzards and deer and red kites as I cycle to work in the morning, not just when I get a notion to 'return to nature'.

So let's play merry hell with the distinctions between what counts as wild and what counts as human, between what's condemned as a visual obscenity and what's seen as a marvel of the age. Let's mess up the boundaries and get a new measure of ourselves as a species. Wind farms, in the right places, don't have to stand between industry and what we still like to think of as wild nature. They can pay their aesthetic, ethical and ecological dues by helping to fund conservation and reintroduction projects. The path to the renewable energy sources of the future can also become, if we invest enough thought and money, a path to a new, richer experience of those other lives with whom we share the planet.

The sun has all but disappeared behind Uamh Bheag and I decide to head back to Doune before night falls. Once I'm through the wind farm gates I quit pedalling and freewheel downhill in the shimmery evening light. The grass bends and sways in the wind. Some sheep run ahead of me for a few yards then swerve off the track and plunge into swathes of tall, thick bracken. I can hear the fizzy trilling of meadow pipits but the sky isn't graced by the broad, silent wings of red kites – just a few rooks and crows. I don't mind. We share the same bit of earth – the wind, the turbines, the red kites and me. We're all part of the mix, part of the overlap. Right now that feels like a good thing to know.

★ ★ ★

With thanks to Lynn and Tom Bowser of Argaty Red Kites, and to Kevin Duffy of the Scottish Raptor Study Group.

Native

JIM CARRUTH

MY BROTHER'S CLOUD

This low-lying cumulus
circling the farm with its shadow
is here because in the last few years

you didn't take a gun to the heart of its dance,
chase it away, instead fed it: that careful spilling
at the edge of troughs, until it's a thousand voices.

It does not threaten rain nor is a sign of anything
other than acceptance, so I catch you looking up
in your all-too-full days to lose yourself

in its endless shape-shifting,
in its heartbeat-fluttering
lustre of murmuration

as you spiral, swoop,
drop, perch, rest,
alight.

ROE

I wasn't tracking, rather
saw you by chance in the clearing

but I love fresh snowfall in the forest
following the journeys of others –

refugees from the chill northerlies
foraging for grass, leaves, berries.

Between the trees the first flash of white
a heart-shaped rump, tense lithe body of doe.

You raise your head skywards
black nose, large ears alert to clues.

Winter has taken away your gold-red coat
left you dull brown, short hair rippled by ribs.

Now fully grown, how small your kind remain.
A short life too – first spotted a few years ago,

a sleeping fawn leaning on your mother,
you will not see out ten years in this wood.

Soon I'll walk here with your absence
but what does that mean for us today?

One of us is too frightened to move
for what they sense but cannot see

the other scared to breathe for fear
of losing what they have right now.

PLANTING ASPEN SAPLINGS

Planting aspen saplings
father and son

though I might not live to see
them grow to full height

their grey bark covered in lichen
flowering catkins in the spring

or listen to their leaves tremble
at the slightest breeze.

Son, you are quick to speak
of this native's decline

that this is where they belong –
a wet moorland on the west.

You talk too of the nature of its roots
the unseen suckers underneath

how colonies from a single seed
can endure a thousand years

even sending up new trunks
in a forest fire's charred aftermath.

You tell me of the tree's offer
to gall midges, birds, hare, deer

the importance of relationships
the interconnectedness of everything.

They do not thrive in shade, need light
and space to grow.

Planting aspen saplings
father and son.

HARVEST OF THE BONE CAVES

i. **Lower Jawbone of Arctic Lemming**
   (lemming geal − 10,000 years old)

The desire to survive
has driven her kind to hide
deep in the winter burrows
of a land smothered by snow.

In a nest of feathers and grass
this tiny tunnel-digger feeds
on the diminished store of seeds
gleaned from a harvest past.

Spring brings her above ground
to nibble new shoots, lichens, roots.
When her whitened fur turns brown
the arctic fox will follow suit,

picking up the scent, acting on
the urgency to mate and spawn.

JIM CARRUTH

ii. **Skull of Northern Lynx**
(Lioncs Tuathach – 1,770 years old)

Contouring an early thaw,
she hunches low;
her huge webbed paws
soft-pad the snow.

With her silver coat,
white-spotted belly,
she is a silent ghost
at the edge of trees.

Stopping in her tracks,
she raises her thick neck,
lifts her small head back,
black ears pricked alert

as the twig-snap of prey
meets the hunger of the day.

iii. **Incisor Tooth of Brown Bear**
  (Mathan donn − *12,000 years old)*

For this thick-haired beast,
this dedicated mother,
it has been about the feast –
months gorging for another.

Summer berries, leaves,
gathering in all she can seize,
building up her reserves
for the child in her belly.

Now it's about staying warm,
conserving precious heat
in a cave safe from storms,
that slowing of her heartbeat.

A bear readied for winter,
the cub curled inside her.

iv. **Reindeer Antler Fragments**
   *(*Rèin-fhiadh – *25,000 years old)*

Sensing the long snows
are almost at an end,
that there's new growth
in the grass in the glen,

the herd will drop down,
seeking this greening pasture –
ancient calving grounds
on the valley floor.

There the challenge of birth:
to spawn then safeguard
their young's first days on earth,
knowing survival will be hard.

The mothers watch it all,
each unsteady step and fall.

v. **Lower Jaw of Wolf**
   (Madadh allaidh – 10,000 years old)

Some wolves remain alone
at the death of their mate,
carrying them in their bones
like a never-ending wake.

Those who come across
this outsider of the pack,
still so angry at her loss,
should be wary of attack

for she is hackles raised
on winter fur, she is fang
and claw at lightning pace,
the whole snarling shebang.

Strange mix of threat and fear:
she does not want you here.

The Wasps' Byke

JACQUELINE BAIN

S cotland is sizzling in the tropical temperatures of a
continental heatwave, and early-morning sunshine
has painted the house walls Tuscany yellow. In my small
triangle of garden-meadow, wildflowers nod lethargic-
ally, heads bowed, as if praying for monsoon rains to
come.

It's the kind of day in which in the past I'd have slung
binoculars around my neck and whistled on Bonny, my
Border Collie. We'd head off to the Gleniffer Braes, an
upland area of moor and woodland visible from my
bedroom window beyond the rooftops opposite.

But that was in a previous life. I no longer have the
mobility to roam the Braes and Bonny isn't here any
more. Instead, I sit motionless on the stone bench,
watching a wasps' byke. The wasps have made their
home in the ornamental doocot, a replica that could
pass as a real one but for the pigeonholes that are small
and round. Not big enough for a sparrow to squeeze

through, never mind a dove, but perfect, it seems, for these dinky, dapper critters.

I have a good view of them without being too close for comfort; the circular entrance hole is clearly visible from my lower vantage point. The wasps are not interested in me though. In ones and twos, they pause momentarily and wiggle their antennae, before launching from the byke like airgun pellets.

The byke was well underway by the time I noticed it a few days ago. Fossil-grey papier mâché bulges from the seams of a pigeonhole. Right now two wasps are on guard duty, one on top of the hole and the other underneath. Both face the byke, making sure only same-community workers fly in and out.

I harbour a secret, internal, motherly sense of pride. I had noticed wasps sooking the weather-bleached fence, chewing wood fibres and mashing them to a pulpy paste with saliva. Now that the garden is a construction site too I see things in a whole new light.

The queen wasp selected the doocot as her preferred plot in springtime. Then she would have taken on all roles: estate agent, interior designer and builder. She'd have laid her eggs in hexagon-shaped cells, and they would have hatched into grubs, becoming the all-female workforce I see going back and forth. In turn they took over byke construction and grub feeding, allowing their queen to focus purely on egg production.

From now on, over the summer months, the byke will increase in size and the colony will multiply, and keep going until the queen dies when the weather gets colder.

Her newborn princesses (gynes) will mate and head off into hibernation, and the remaining female workers and drones (males) will all die off.

I know this because the wasps' byke is making something stir inside me: long-buried memories. It takes me back to a time when I was about seven or eight years old. That little person appears inside, reminding me that I once had a kinship with wasps. For different reasons, different circumstances, but once more I find myself alone in a dawn garden, gazing at wasps.

I liked wasps when I was very young, but then I inherited spheksophobia, a fear of wasps that was cultural, taught to me, and I learned to jump up and down and flap and shriek like everyone else. This lasted for a long time until one day I heard Bill Oddie on TV, saying that wasps were good garden pollinators and pest-controllers, an important part of the ecosystem. My whole attitude changed and my fears vanished into thin air. But even in my years of fervent wasp-unease, I didn't believe they deserved the inhumanity meted out to them during their short, seasonal lives: swatted, sprayed with chemicals, hair-spray and vinegar, squashed and drowned. It all seemed so cruel and unnecessary.

In the council-house garden of my childhood, jars of jam and water to attract wasps were placed at strategic points by my mum, who wouldn't normally hurt a fly. Corpses piled on top of submerged corpses, turning crisp and curly, filling the jars to the brim until they were tipped out on bin day. I once asked my mum the reason for the mass destruction.

'They're a nuisance, evil. Sting for no reason other than nastiness.'

The simplicity of the answer mystified me. Manky Morag McLeod with frizzy pigtails and buck teeth, who lived across the road, nipped, kicked, bit, slapped and scratched for no other reason than nastiness, but nobody suggested sticking her in a glass jar to meet a jammy end.

One evening I got into a fight with Morag because she said I'd been wearing the same pants, unwashed, for two weeks. Legs entwined, arms fangled, we had a grip of each other's hair and were glued together in a physically induced impasse.

'I'll let go if you do,' she said, breathless and grunting.

I let go and she didn't.

I limped home, sobbing, my shins a mountain range of blue and purple peaks. The only response I got was an unsympathetic 'Well, stay away from her then'.

It was around that time I developed an unspoken and private empathy with the struggling, dying creatures in the jam jars and, unknown to Mum, began to scoop live ones out with a feather.

Of course, I know now that wasps don't sting out of nastiness. Being stung is a painful and unpleasant experience, and is perhaps the key reason for wasps being one of our most unpopular insects. The pain is caused by a cocktail of toxic pheromones, produced in venom glands, and secreted into the stinger when it plunges into prey or perceived and real threats.

Only females sting. The stinger is a biologically complicated organ, a modified ovipositor (a tube-like tool used by insects to lay eggs). Some species of wasp still use this method when injecting eggs into their victims.

For the kind of wasps in my doocot byke, the stinger has been adapted as a defence mechanism, and is used by females to defend the byke and its occupants. We fear their sting so we destroy their bykes. In late summer, colonies stop breeding new workers and the existing ones are on the lookout for nectar-rich, sugary food – they pester us, wanting to share our strawberry tarts and glasses of wine. Their presence gets us into a tizzy; the commotion annoys and imperils the wasps – and the stingers are at the ready.

In this country their second biggest threat is badgers, who do not eat the adults but will dig out a byke to feast on the maggot-like larvae.

My doocot wasps are safe from badgers, and as I sit in the sun, increasingly entertained by their comings and goings, I vow to keep them as safe as possible from human disruption and let them live out their allocated lifecycle in peace.

So it's while I'm sitting here on the hot stone bench that a plan comes to mind to create a wasp-feeding station. There's an old chopping board in the kitchen that I can sit on top of the compost bin to make a level surface. The compost bin is tucked away, so the wasp's flight path will be segregated from the hub of the garden.

I'll supply jam, strawberry and raspberry, a basic brand. It won't just keep them out of the way, it's an atonement for the carnage inflicted on their ancestors in my childhood garden.

There are about nine thousand species of wasp in the UK, belonging to the scientific order Hymenoptera, a group of insects named principally because of their membrane-like, transparent wings.

I am pretty sure 'mine' are common wasps, *Vespula vulgaris*, a small-sized breed, banded with yellow and black stripes, with saffron legs, long antennae and a complex visual arrangement made up of two compound eyes and several triangular ocelli that gives them excellent detection of movement.

I picture the queen coming out of hibernation in springtime to forage among speckles of early primrose, lesser celandine and wood anemone. Every year, I wait expectantly for my first queen bumblebee sighting and highlight it in my nature journal. Not so the queen wasp, but next year will be different.

As the morning wears on, drapes of undulating hot air fall to earth and rise back up, meeting in the middle as a flamingo-pink haze. An eruption of weary blackbird song ceases, and drum-beats of bumblebee wings are muted by foxglove bells. Only I and the wasps seem to be alive and breathing in our own, shared, quiet and timeless landscape. The workers that zoomed in and out of the byke in ones and twos now hurry back and forth in silent squadrons.

Yesterday, I watched a solitary wasp drag a grub across the garden path, my first and only encounter with such a thing. It hauled the pearly-grey larva for a few milli-metres and then paused, jiggling its antennae and giving its rainbow, stained-glass wings an impatient, sunny shake. I had no idea what species the larva was, whether it was the wasp's own grub or one it planned to parasitise. I began to mull over the lone wasp compared to the social community in the byke, which would, soon swell in number to hundreds and possibly even thousands. Some species of solitary wasp will nest in small groups with their own kind, but each one maintains responsibility for their own offspring, and they do not have the sophisti-cated societal roles of the byking wasps.

Both styles of living make perfect sense to me; socia-bleness and solitude are features of my personality I've never really been able to reconcile. Early on in life, I felt different and uncomfortable in company, other than with my family. The natural world was where I fitted in; I've loved wildlife for as long as I can remember. The outdoor continuum of textures, tastes, scents, patterns and colours fascinated me. Nature gripped my senses and attention, and made me forget injustices like those doled out by Manky Morag McLeod.

That childhood garden was untidy and hazy with cloying scents of blackcurrant and raspberry bushes. I hunted for ladybirds, beetles and caterpillars, talking to them in the same way my sister communicated with her Sindy dolls.

I withdrew more and more into the wild landscapes of nature and my mind, and rescuing wasps from death-trap jam jars became my guilty secret. I remained in that world until I was about nineteen, when the pressure to be 'normal' took over.

As I got older I became aware that my solitude and interest in bugs and beasties was considered strange. Most of us are expected to grow out of an insect hobby as we are told that the things that fascinate our juvenile minds are dirty, malevolent and dangerous, and are subsequently wiped clean from our lives by swatters and detergents. Gender also played a huge part for me, as it wasn't considered the norm for girls to be interested in bugs, mud-crawling and tree-climbing.

I pulled my solitary, natural self out of my body, threw it down, and marched off into the future, not looking back. I stumbled through life, shying from emotion and generally making a mess of things. During my 'social years' I never lost interest in the natural world, but progressed from insects to larger mammals such as foxes and badgers.

But when my mobility deteriorated I had to re-evaluate my relationship with nature and get to know the creatures that were willing to come to me.

The scorching weather continues. A yellow-ochre glow covers the Braes where I used to walk. Lots of wasps zip to and from the byke. I am content watching them. It feels good; it feels right. Like the wasps, I can just get on with things, and I no longer care if people think I'm weird. Nature is struggling and I want to help. I'm strong enough to admit I like wasps and am looking out for them. I am back in the comfort zone of my natural self. I have stuffed it back inside and won't dump it ever again. I never found normality in the 'normal' world.

The byke has brought me back to who I really am. Not a little girl any more but an adult who has redis-covered an inside wild space that welcomes wasps. I perch on the farthest reaches where imagination and reality combine to give me a new yet familiar sense of self.

Life has come full circle. It is fun being a born-again wasper!

Bones of the Forth

GAVIN FRANCIS

But who knows the fate of his bones, or how often he is to be buried? Who hath the oracle of his ashes, or whither they are to be scattered?
Sir Thomas Browne, *Urn Burial*

There's an appeal to the phrase 'Firth of Forth', to its alliteration, the neat swivel of vowels, the way it bridges the descriptive geography of 'firth' with the toponymic 'Forth' in a soft roll and tap of the tongue. There's an echo there of the froth of the sea, the thrift of the shore, of birth, of going forth. On maps of Scotland the firth is easy to find: that southernmost gash in the country's eastern shoreline – so smooth in comparison with the exploded mosaic of islands in the west. It's the coast of rich farms and richer oilfields, of herring villages and mining towns, of university cities braced against Scandinavian winds. The Forth cuts into it all like a polished knife.

As a child growing up in Fife it seemed an immense body of water, a division between continents. I'd glimpse it from the boles of climbed trees, from hilltop picnics, the colours of its water shifting with the circuit of the sun and the restlessness of the clouds: silver, cobalt, lead, copper. An anchor in the landscape, tethering my sense of place. Once I sought it out in an atlas chart comparing the rivers of the world, but was disappointed: such a meagre thread beside the Volga, the Rhine, even the Severn. But to restore the dignity of the river it was enough to put down the atlas and walk a few yards from the house – fields and forests cascaded in slow, geological waves down to the shore at the Rosyth Naval Dockyard, at that time, the early 1980s, among Fife's biggest employers. Edinburgh and the Pentland Hills beyond the river appeared impossibly distant, and the world they shielded – of England, Europe, the globe – unimaginable. This was the way the world was meant to be, its contours moulded somewhere deep into my growing sense of self: woodland and barleyfield, the sun's arc from North Sea in the east to the Trossachs in the west, and beneath it all, the glitter of the Firth of Forth.

A web of pilgrim routes extends invisibly over the Forth: South Queensferry to North; Cramond to Aberdour; North Berwick to Elie. There are medieval chapels at each of those pilgrims' harbours and on most of the islands, or 'Inches', of the Forth. Among the largest of those islands is the May, about five miles offshore. It's a mile long and a third of a mile wide: a great volcanic sill of greenstone thrust out between 250 and 300 million years ago when Scotland was desert, its tectonic bedrock drifting somewhere just north of the equator.

The medieval chapel on the May is built on a raised

beach – Scotland is even now rebounding from the burden of its last glaciation – and there's a mound there of burials dating all the way back to the retreat of the Romans and Christianity's arrival in the fifth or sixth centuries. But with such abundant and reliable birdlife it would be odd if the island hadn't been visited over millennia prior to that, for eggs and meat. We don't know which of the many peoples who've belonged here granted the name 'May': it could be Norse ('Gull Island'), Gaelic ('flat, a plain'), or Pictish (the tribe north of the Antonine Wall being known as the Maeatae). There's evidence of human settlements along the Forth going back at least six thousand years.

The May is special to me because I knew it as a child from holidays in the east of Fife, and a few years ago I went to live there on a sort of pilgrimage of my own. I'd had enough of living in the city, and during a spell of frenetic work in Edinburgh applied to spend a few weeks there as a volunteer warden, joining the ornithologists and conservationists who monitor the island's seabirds. My first evening on the island I sat out on the thrift listening to thousands of kittiwakes and gulls calling to one another in the westering sunlight. Skirts of rainfall swept over the East Neuk to the north, while to the south the volcanic plug of the Bass Rock shone, like a nail God had neglected to hammer all the way in.

One of the tasks I was given was to dig out the old well from which the medieval chapel once drew its water, water renowned in the middle ages as a restorer of fertility.

I spent a couple of days in the pit of the well, chucking out spadefuls of thin, sandy soil, rotten seaweed, the bones of dead seabirds, until I stood on a deck of pebbles, water sloshing at the tops of my wellies. The chapel itself was excavated by a team of archaeologists under Peter Yeoman in the 1990s, and appears to have been an early medieval infirmary: the skeletons in its graveyard displayed an unusually high rate of illness and trauma, as if pilgrims once travelled to the island to be healed. An archaeologist called Marlo Willows recently completed a study of the skeletons, assessing their illnesses and injuries.

In the evenings it became my habit to make a circuit of the cliffs; from my bunkroom in the lighthousekeepers' cottages, west to that crest of greenstone, along the rooftops of cities of seabirds, then south to the cape, past the chapel and the pilgrims' well. There was something timeless about the place – its ancient bedrock, the swing of its seasons, the gulls, guillemots and puffins. Though dominant species of seabirds have come and gone over the centuries (much as Romans, Picts and Norse have come and gone) there's comfort in the knowledge that the seasonal coming and going of the birds went on for millennia before I was born, and will go on for millennia after me.

From the southern tip of the island it's possible to see the Lothian shore as it curves westwards to Edinburgh, and south-east towards Berwick. You can make out the white Lego brick of Torness Power Station, one of two working nuclear power stations in Scotland. It's a new addition, commissioned in 1987. Watching it day after day, I began to wonder how much radioactivity leaches from it into the bones of the Forth's fish, birds and humans. If we're spared, as a species, to live along the Forth for another six thousand years, what will people then make of our own middens, graves and bones?

The image of the Torness Power Station stayed with me. Later, I looked it up on the website of Scotland's Environmental Protection Agency, SEPA: 'Discharges of authorised liquid radioactive wastes are made to the Firth of Forth', it said. Contaminants from the nuclear reactor are found within the shellfish along the shoreline, but at 'safe concentrations': radioactive isotopes of strontium, manganese, cobalt, copper, caesium and tritium – a weakly radioactive form of hydrogen. 'Concentrations of artificial radionuclides were mainly due to the distant effects of Sellafield discharges', it said, as if in reassurance – drifted here all the way from the Irish Sea – 'and to weapon testing and Chernobyl fallout'.

Some of those isotopes may have leaked from the dockyard at Rosyth, upstream beyond the iconic road and rail bridges. Rosyth was a Polaris then a Trident nuclear submarine base until recently, and seven old subs still lie sleeping in its waters. The work of decommissioning has been repeatedly postponed as another generation's problem, but is reportedly now tentatively underway; too expensive to dismantle safely, too dangerous to forget, we've been arguing as a nation what to do with the submarines for longer now than they were ever in service. I clicked on the SEPA report for Rosyth: 'The site is authorised to discharge gaseous radioactive waste in addition to the discharge of liquid radioactive waste through an outfall into the Firth of Forth.' The private contractors who manage the submarines have a licence to dispose of radioactive cobalt and tritium directly into the water, and carbon and tritium isotopes into the air. 'Concentrations of radionuclides from the site remain extremely low', said the report. Radioactive caesium has also been detected, but at 'levels anticipated from histor-ical nuclear weapons testing fallout'.

My thinking about the bones of the Forth persisted. Back in the 1990s, those skeletons excavated from the Isle of May had been cleaned on site, boxed up and transported by boat to Crail on the East Neuk coast, then by road to Glasgow for analysis. After a few years they were moved to a museum depot at South Queensferry. Recently they were moved from there to another museum depot at Granton, just a few miles along the Forth coast. I went to Granton on another pilgrimage of sorts, to be met by Dr Alice Blackwell, curator of Medieval Archaeology, who'd had the courtesy, generosity and curiosity to reply to my questions about the human remains from the May.

The store she welcomed me to was as big as a leisure centre, with the same whitewashed breezeblock walls and echoing steel stairwells. But appearances, as ever, were deceptive: the store revealed itself as a house of wonders. Alice led me past industrial shelving units stacked with antique spinning wheels, sequestered there as if from *Sleeping Beauty*; series of Roman amphorae, lolling on custom-built mounts; a 3D-printed, Neolithic skull; rows upon rows of medieval cauldrons.

Much of the collections are shelved on rolling racks; Alice birled the handles and the shelves sprang apart to the ones concerning the Isle of May: floor to ceiling stacks of buff cardboard boxes filled with pottery, metal, medieval roof tiles, animal bones. She pulled a few down and we went through them: an amber bead, ironworked door latches, bits of butchered bone, stones that look as if they've been worked by hand – the detritus of everyday life, grown strange with age. In one box was a scallop shell, found placed in the mouth of a buried pilgrim as a final sacrament. A strange custom, I thought; then again, these were communities sustained by the sea. The scallops of the Forth all now carry a radioactive taint.

Human remains are accorded deeper respect than animal bones and are stored in a separate space. An oste-ologist had sifted through and accorded them special status. Unlike other archaeological finds, they can't legally be owned.

'What a place!' I said. 'Was it built specially to contain all this?'

'Oh yes, all custom built,' said Alice. 'But there's no Wi-Fi or computer points where you actually need them. Ah! Here they are.' We were in a space halfway between a room and a cupboard. Sea light fell into it from a window in the north-east, the direction of the May island. 'Which ones are you after again?'

Carbon dating of the human remains on the May testify to burials over more than a millennium: thirteen of the excavated skeletons turned out to have lived between 400 and 600 A.D., when its first chapel would have been built. Isotopes of carbon revealed the age of these individuals, but radioisotopes of oxygen, nitrogen and strontium indicate what kind of foods they ate, and where they grew up. Strontium is permanently embedded into tooth enamel as it forms, and so ratios of strontium isotopes in the teeth can point to where someone was living as their adult teeth came in.

'Can we see the box for 859?' I asked. According to Marlo Willows' research, 859 contained the skeleton of a man who'd suffered prostate cancer.

He was middle-aged, and had died in the sixth or seventh century A.D. – his still-sturdy bones were speckled with seedlings of tumours. Strontium analysis revealed that he seemed to have come to the May from somewhere in central Scotland, west of the source of the Forth. We turned over the bones, yellowed with age, examining the roughened bone rosettes of the cancer that likely killed him. Then silently we packed them away again with care; I wondered at the rituals that accompanied his first interment. 'And 997?' I asked. The skeleton in 997 was of a teenaged boy, also dead in the sixth or seventh century, his spine distorted by what was probably congenital tuberculosis and his leg bones hollowed from disuse. The enamel of his teeth suggested he'd grown up nearby.

'Any others?' Alice asked.

'Can we see 972?'

Alice lowered another buff cardboard box down to me; 972 contained a later medieval burial, from the fourteenth or fifteenth century, also with a twisted spine. Reckoned to be aged only seven or eight at death, he or she was so stunted by chronic illness that the bones seemed of a much younger child. The spine Alice held was fragile, fused – this child would have had to be carried everywhere, and would not have survived even seven or eight years without close and loving care. As we turned the bones in our hands, delicate as parchment, we talked about the depth of suffering this child endured, the desperation his or her parents must have felt; whether he or she was taken to the Isle of May to die, to be buried, or to be healed. How faith infused every element of medieval life, and how their Christian faith implied belief in the resurrection of these very bones.

'How old are your kids?' Alice asked me.

'About this age,' I replied.

'Mine too.'

And we spoke of fear for the future, of faith and doubt in human progress, of the hostility of a world that will see all of us returned to dust and bone.

★

If my own bones, or the bones of my children – also children of the Firth of Forth – are ever pulled from the earth and analysed, the archaeologists of the future will have no problem locating us to the late twentieth and early twenty-first centuries. If my femur is ever pulverised and its dust analysed, a line of caesium-137 will be revealed – an isotope that doesn't exist naturally, introduced worldwide with the weapons testing of the 1950s and 1960s. The food chains of our planet are saturated with it now. Man-made radioactive contamination is today so ubiquitous that to build Geiger counters and aeronautical sensors it's necessary to scavenge steel from old shipwrecks, built in what now seems a time of innocence, before the nuclear age.

Other, more exotic, isotopes were released in the Chernobyl meltdown, and so those future scientists might be able to place me as a northern European, whose bones were on the threshold of puberty that spring in 1986 when a radioactive cloud swept north and west from Ukraine, reaching the Firth of Forth on the second day of May.

It's not difficult to imagine some future technology able to distinguish the radioactive signature of the Fukushima disaster, something that occurred when my children were babies, their bones and teeth growing rapidly. Fukushima discharged radioactive caesium, iodine and tellurium into the Pacific, isotopes that have since been detected everywhere around the world's coasts, having circulated on ocean currents.

Sometimes when I take the kids down to the beach,

and join them skiddling and paddling in the water, I look up to see the cranes and hangars that stand over the submarines of Rosyth Dockyard. In those moments it's not fanciful to imagine that, in the analysis of our bones, some archaeologists of the future may be able to locate our family as having lived for many years in the region once known as Lothian. Isotopes peculiar to the operation of nuclear submarines will be revealed, and I wonder how they'll characterise that long-abandoned technology. 'An archaic, largely military technology of the twentieth and twenty-first centuries,' they'll say, 'rapidly obsolete, because of the risk it posed to human life.' Perhaps they'll puzzle over why a densely populated river estuary was chosen to stockpile some of the most insidious and enduring poisons it has been our culture's folly to devise, and our shame.

The Lurgies

LESLEY HARRISON

THE LURGIES, MONTROSE BASIN

'It is a fallacy to suppose that the music of the wild bird is unprogressive . . . The fact is, the bird has not arrived.'

F. Schuyler Mathews,
Field Book of Wild Birds and Their Music

'Birdsong is continually evolving into this place.'
Andy and Peter Holden, *Natural Selection*
Arbroath Old Courthouse, April–May 2019

song thrush
    x3 repeats
    x4 with subtle
    x5 lengthening, or *tremolo*

gob, gub, gebbie, gab, goggie
    an unfledged bird.

kwink / pinkfoot
    runic.
    descending
    out of pink skies.

dunnock
    a sub song,
    full of ornament.
    a choir of one.

teuchie, teuchit, chewit, tee whip, wep
    peewit.

heron
    skreik – a grinding
    locomotive piston.
    the creaking of pulleys

arctic tern
    a tirrick.
    its sound magnifies in colder air.

willow warbler
   rosy, aerial.
   the music of clouds

hoodie craw
   a hacking cough.
   it demoralises all nests in its territory.

wren
   in dry scrub –
   a music box.

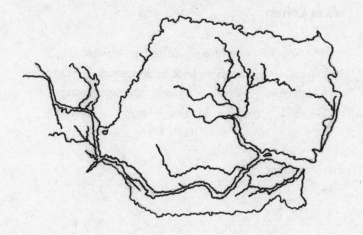

ephemera   of insects, flowers etc.: existing only for one
day

seeps   expulsion of shallow gas from ancient plant
matter

swatter   to flutter or splash in water

spink   a bird note

WATERSHED

– pow – lemno – quharity – prosen –
– farthal – gourach – leck – loupshiel – cluthie –
– fafernie – gowal – style – moulzie – capel –
– cald – rottal – kinrive – noran – briech –

LESLEY HARRISON

LUNAN

the bald dunes.
the bare east light.
the *this* of the ocean.

THE CADGERS' ROAD

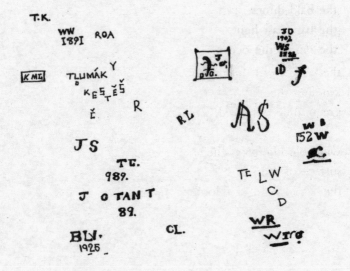

LESLEY HARRISON

THE RED HEAD

standing on the cliff
towards Denmark,

the wind from the moon
kindling the sky
green, then coral red,

wind blooming on the
surface of the sea.
the sea in constant bloom

AUCHMITHIE

the bus stop
    a thuggish wind
    hurls car lights round the corner,
    the road out marbled with snow.

Margaret's garden
    a garden of
    sudden small birds
    arriving, mute from their journey.

the Mains
    walking in the hare light of June,
    the North Sea dark behind the houses

the cart track
    differing weather.
    a blue boat
    pulled high on the turf.

Back End
    Force 9.
    my house creaks like a ship at sea.
    in the morning, seaweed on the pavement.

St Vigeans
    rain blows through
    like the long, deep breath of a whale

    each bird in its alcove.
    a cross and a spiral
    a deer carved still

Three Meditations on Absence
in Nature and Life

CHITRA RAMASWAMY

POLL DOMHAIN

Looking back from the vantage point of right now, it occurs to me that the walks we don't do might be as significant as the ones we do. The roads not so much less travelled as not travelled at all. After all, absences matter in nature as much as they do in life. Recesses, glens and corries are as much a part of 'the total mountain', as Nan Shepherd so satisfyingly called it, as its ridges, braes and summits.

I am thinking, specifically, of a walk I failed to do in the late spring of 2017 when I was seven months pregnant with my second child. We were staying in Applecross, that most contained and possessively loved of Scotland's peninsulas, as much because of how it's reached as what you find when you get there. And how it is reached! Via the Bealach na Bà, an historic drover's road criss-crossing the mountains with the precocity of a rhythm gymnast's ribbon. A dizzying sequence of hairpin bends more alpine than Scottish in spirit and gradient, it seems old to us but is as close as our last breath next to the millions of years the mountain has on it. The Bealach, by comparison, was laid in 1822, the same year the Caledonian Canal, linking Scotland's east and west coasts through the Great Glen, was completed. Walter Scott's 'land of the mountain and the flood' was opening up to the world. To people, cattle and to the bold (and entitled) Victorian idea of touring. Of going places, just for the sake of being in them.

Almost two hundred years later we pitched up. This was not long after the latest tourist drive had taken off with a verve and, some might say, shortsightedness to match the Victorians. The North Coast 500: billed as 'the ultimate road trip around Scotland' and sponsored by – who else? – Aston Martin, with the promise of 'the best dolphin viewpoint in Scotland!' and watching 'salmon leap upstream!' Included within the 516-mile loop was the Bealach na Bà and so for the first time driving that notorious single-track road we shared it with a cavalcade of bikers, endurance cyclists, motorhomes and petrol-heads in classic cars. My feelings were mixed. As Shepherd noted of her beloved Cairngorms in the 1977 foreword to *The Living Mountain*, written thirty years after she first penned the masterpiece, 'too many boots, too much commotion, but then how much uplift for how many hearts'. Later, a local who ran a small farm shop out of his garage told me that accidents were on the rise, and the Bealach was unable to withstand the traffic. Not for the first time, though perhaps the first in Scotland, I wondered if the best way to love a place was to not go there at all.

We rented a crofter's cottage (clad in more wood panelling than I had ever seen) called 'the house on the rocks'. This was to be the location of our last holiday as the three of us, four including the dog, though of course the fifth was there too, orbiting my womb and growing in size and insistence by the day. There was a farm opposite and one warm afternoon our dog, as foolishly urbane as her owners, escaped and chased the sheep and spring lambs until the farmer's wife bellowed at her to 'GO HOME!', a top-of-the-voice order that reverberated across the higgledy-piggledy township of Toscaig – where we never saw another soul – and probably reached the spider crabs twitching in the bay around the disused harbour. The dog instantly obeyed, returning to us with her tail between her legs. My son, then three and terrified of the drone of the 'buzzy bees having their breakfast' in the garden, a fear which bloomed that summer and has made a seasonal return every year since, was so taken with the drama he ventured outside to jump up and down and laugh his head off. We admonished him because it wasn't funny (though our mouths were beginning to twitch in the way of parents doing their best to remain parents under humorous circumstances). And it wasn't. But there was a hysteria to those long, close days in that cottage clinging to the rocks and in the end we laughed too. The bees continued their floral song, but we did not hear it.

The following day we decided to attempt a nearby walk to the coral beach at Ard Ban. Just six kilometres on an ancient path through moorland and coast. We read the instructions on our phones as if we were different people, or rather our former selves. Perhaps it was an act of wish fulfilment; those desire lines making for the land's edge represented who we wanted to be in a time of escalating responsibility, with more of everything on the way. Basically, we read them as if we were free. To go where we liked, when we wanted, at a pace of our choosing. Walking an existing route is often, paradoxically, about the pursuit of a designated amount of freedom. The freedom to be told where to go and how precisely to get there. To follow obtuse signs on wooden posts knocked into the ground. To intuit nothing beyond what part of a path to give your weight. To refresh screen-dry eyes with horizons, natural light (as we now call what was once just light) and living things, large and small, real and imagined, flitting on the periphery of your vision. To pick up a pebble just to carry it, warm, in the hollow of your hand.

The reality? Two women, one heavily pregnant. A four-year-old boy on the brink of massive change: a sister and, a fortnight after her birth, an autism diagnosis. And an anxious city dog overwhelmed by unfamiliar scents. The sky was overcast, which combined with my desic-cated eyes (was the foetus drinking from them too?) made it difficult to see. It was as if the world had resolved into an under-exposed photograph. It had been raining all morning and the stony paths ran with rivulets of very clear, glossy water. As the moorland became more boggy, the pools on either side of the path, which seemed like a bridge suspended over water, became swollen. Irregular drops plopped into them, proof that it was still raining even if we could not feel it. My son, already demanding to be carried on my partner's shoulders, preferably back to the car, became obsessed with these 'muddy puddles'. He would not be moved on. Everywhere there was water – and this being Wester Ross moorland there was nowhere water was not – had to be paid tribute by way of a stone thrown into its cloudy depths. When a stone could not be prised from the path with his small cold fingers, my son railed at the injustice.

Meanwhile, my pelvic girdle, that butterfly-shaped cluster of bones pinned to the mouth of the spine, was killing me, producing a rhythmic grinding when I walked that felt as though it would be ground to dust in the same way a dead butterfly's wings crumble to nothing. Every time I had to step wide or come down on unstable ground, or go downhill, or uphill for that matter, it hurt. Everywhere there was oppression: in the sky, my body and the tense atmosphere between us. Finally I refused to continue and sat on a rock overlooking a small sheltered bay studded by a single outcrop of rock where one immediately pictured seals basking, though there were none. The tide was low and the sky's reflection blackened the water and browned the spiny seaweed in the bay, which I later discovered was called Poll Domhain. Claire, my partner, walked on to see how far this extraordinary coral beach was and whether it was 'worth it', which was unlikely unless my own bed happened to be stranded on the sand. I watched my son, by this time throwing handful after handful of stones into the bay in an ecstasy of permission. I wept half-heartedly. Took a photo on my phone. I consciously tried to look at what was in front of my eyes but my mind had already taken flight, ascending over coast, peninsula and mountain pass until the map of the entire island was revealed with all its divisions, turmoil and extreme weather. The land that was Britain in the maddening weeks leading up to a general election and the horror of the Grenfell fire. I saw myself, a British Indian woman and her son at a remote anchorage point on the north-west fringe of Scotland. It is often in such vulnerable moments that I feel the brown of my skin most viscerally.

Then Claire came back. She had lost faith too, which basically marks the end of a happy walk, and declared the beach too far away. She had not gone far enough to see it herself. We turned back, defeated, but also aware that we had wished for more of the world than we could handle that day.

Three months later, in those wild domestic weeks after a baby is born and a mother's body is made of fluid, fire, and is somehow, like 'the total mountain', itself again, I Googled the area while breastfeeding my daughter in bed. On a walking website I found a photo of Poll Domhain, composed exactly like the one I had taken, almost certainly from the same rock. The only difference was the weather: monochrome in mine, a perfect summer's day in theirs. Apparently just around the corner, on a path bending to the left, was Ard Ban, a trio of abandoned crofts by a coral beach. Though nothing is what it seems and the 'coral' is in fact maerl, fragments of calcified seaweed crushed to a fine powder by the sea, just as I had imagined that walk pounding my pelvis to dust. The sun bleaches the maerl, turning many of western Scotland's beaches a misleading tropical white. Carbon dating has shown that maerl deposits can be more than 5,500 years old. And never mind a nine-month gestation. Maerl grows at a stately pace of a millimetre a year.

I have not been back. Yet the walk to Ard Ban that I did not complete, the destination at which I never arrived, is as powerful a memory as many places I have been. I can even imagine, at some fleet-footed time in the future when I intend – or rather hope – to be more free again, seeing myself on that beach as if I did make it all the way to the land's edge. In fact, there I am now. A temporary home for two people in a land I no longer understand. Sifting centuries-old maerl through my fingers. As foreign and fragile as I'll ever be.

II

PIGEON

When my son was about two years old we lived on a busy thoroughfare in Leith. Our flat was directly opposite a police station and my son liked to stand at the windows and watch the cars parked outside, especially when they turned on their sirens and sped away. The wind that swooped up that street, casting gulls over the rooftops in great arcs, came straight off the Firth of Forth. In winter it was cold enough to draw instant tears from my eyes and made the street lamps attached to our old building waggle like weather vanes. We stood at the window a lot in those long indistinguishable days, so much so that certain neighbours looked up as they passed, expecting to see us and waving when they did. Sometimes I felt ignited by the spark of connection. Sometimes I retreated, embarrassed. Caught in the act of feeling trapped.

One day, as we were standing there, my son watching the cars and me watching the street lamps, a pigeon landed on the windowsill. This was not so unusual. Now and then a pigeon, though never to my knowledge a gull, would briefly alight on our narrow windowsills, which were two floors up above a pub aptly called The Compass. One year, during the winter I discovered I was pregnant with my son, a pigeon nested somewhere near our bathroom window for long enough that even now when I replay the dramatic reveal of that little white stick with its shocking pink plus sign it is accompanied by a warm cooing. But I never saw that pigeon. As the bathroom window was frosted, I only ever heard it. And it was a different time. I was preoccupied with life beyond the walls of my home in those free-as-a-bird days, usually passing through on my way somewhere or other, never homing for long. I did not have children, in other words. That pigeon was incidental. This one, in a time characterised by nothing much happening, was central. It stayed. For well over an hour, which is for ever when you're on toddler (or, one presumes, pigeon) time. So we stayed put too, and time seemed to stand still with us.

I have never paid so much attention to a bird that so many of us see every single day of our lives. A bird threaded so intricately into the fabric of our lives that we have ceased to see it at all. The pigeon must have been injured or stunned to stop for so long but it seemed fine. It appeared not to notice us, and so I was able to spend some time with this descendant of the world's oldest domesticated bird. A species with whom we have co-existed for many thousands of years. A bird that has delivered our messages, fertilised our land, fed us and prompted us to build tiny dome-shaped houses for it all over the Middle East and Europe. I looked deep into this pigeon's left eye, jet black surrounded by a perfect ring of tangerine, and wondered if it looked back at me. Its bobbing neck shone an iridescent green merging into purple, a tropical palette I had never before bothered to admire purely on the grounds that it belonged to a pigeon. The matte grey of its feathers was as true as any shade of Farrow and Ball paint. Observing this pigeon close up, from behind a pane of glass, in the comfort and boredom of my own home, had a similar effect to looking at a found object in a gallery. Taken out of context, its pigeon-ness unfurled. It was the most pigeony pigeon I had ever encountered. This pigeon, a bird routinely written off as a pest even though they rarely transmit diseases to humans, was exceptional. A thing of beauty. A bird worthy of watching.

Becoming a mother does this to you. Sharpens your senses as forcibly as it prises open your heart. It's what looking after children demands of us, and why we are told that we need eyes in the back of our head to do it effectively. Vigilance. A bird's capacity for alertness. So I knew I would need to be attentive to the needs of my son and the hazards around him, but what I did not expect was that my awareness of the non-human world would be heightened too. To parent well, joyously, and with the least amount of conflict is to slow down. To accept that the daisy must be picked, the route deviated from, the gate opened and closed in the rain for all eternity. And when you change your pace, particularly with a person even newer to the planet than you are, you see things all over again.

Yet this person, my person, had never shown any interest in birds. In fact this not caring was so emphatic he didn't seem to even see birds. I always pointed out the mallards, swans and mergansers with their spiky ginger quiffs along the Water of Leith, as parents do with their children, but he never followed the point of my finger. He saw different things: drains, the formation of steps leading down to the river, the dance of sunlight on murky water. He saw specificity, construction, pattern, rather than life. When we tried to feed the birds he ate the bread himself or, if I guided him with my hand, threw it half-heartedly in the water so I knew, in the wordless way mothers just know, that he would rather it were a stone. I was starting to wonder whether all this was a matter of will or capacity. Was he uninterested in birds – which in the flat and judgemental language of childcare is often translated into being *on his own agenda* – or was he seeing the world differently? It was a small thing, but it was there. Like the way he flapped his little brown arms when he was excited as if, indeed, he were a bird. These were reasons, at once humdrum and strange, inarticulable and accumulating like a body of evidence, why I was beginning to think he was autistic. I was frightened, though he was happy, and always so effortlessly and admirably himself. So I began to embrace his interests. To realise that drains could be beautiful too.

This visitation, then, truly was extraordinary. My son not only saw the pigeon, it blew him away. It was as thrilling and unsettling as if Judith Kerr's tiger had come to tea. This was what was required for him to notice a bird. It had to be offered up in a private solo show. It had to be an event outside the norms of daily life. And it had to come to us.

We talked about it, by which I mean my son shouted 'Pigeon!' over and over again and I said 'Yes! Hello pigeon!' and made cucucururuuu noises. We lost interest, wandered away, came back and the pigeon was still there. I became worried and decided to open the window, but before I got the chance, the pigeon flew away. And like the tiger, it never came back.

For many months afterwards my son, whose speech and language continued to develop so idiosyncratically, brought up the pigeon whenever his gaze was drawn to the window. My son, who did not (and, as I was beginning to understand, could not) otherwise talk about the past would repeat the entire conversation, playing both our parts, though not the pigeon. It is a form of speech known as echolalia, a sustained parrot-speak common both in children learning to speak but also an indicator of autism. This unusual and playful way of speaking, which I had never encountered before but fell into so easily, amused me, thrilled me, scared me. It also made perfect sense. It suited my son. It could not be any other way.

The pigeon-talk went on for a very long time. It had been a home-bound adventure. It had opened a channel of desperately longed-for communication between us. For a few months this bird was a major character in the story of our lives. The truth is, I never once stood at that window again without thinking about that pigeon. And the message it brought me.

III
MUDLARKING

The most recent walk I did not do was in London, where I was born and where my parents and sister live. I hesitated to include it in this brief, incomplete history of absences because as soon as the words ventured across the border I feared they exempted themselves from inclusion. But the business of living knows nothing of such boundaries any more than the land shifts according to borders redrawn, backstops contested or walls threatened. I have now spent more than half my life crossing back and forth between Scotland and England, two increasingly riven parts of what I might once have thought of as 'the total country'. Life goes on, from here to there, and I continue to be as at home, and at sea, in both.

This walk I did not do was on my sister's birthday in 2019. She took the day off work – highly unusual in itself for a Londoner – and went to spend it with my parents in south-west London, where they live in a block of council flats, though almost all but my parents' and one or two others are now ex-council. The street runs parallel to the unexpectedly pastoral part of the Thames where the Boat Race finishes. Old trees grow right on the river's edge there, bending damp trunks to the brown tides. Wherever we lived in London when I was growing up, we lived near the Thames, so I have walked these muddy towpaths all my life. And there is no mud quite so ripe and squelchy as Thames mud, with a consistency close to melted chocolate and a smell that, for me, just is home.

Thames mud is nature's own embalmer, containing no oxygen and preserving whatever it consumes. This means the river's foreshore, where my dad used to stand and throw bread to the pigeons, earning himself the local nickname of 'the bird man of Mortlake', is one of the richest archaeological sites in Britain. Sometimes, amongst the dog-walkers, mothers jogging with their upscale three-wheeler buggies and occasional heron, you can spot a lone figure mudlarking along the foreshore. Something Victorians did for a living: picking flotsam and jetsam beside an industrial river seething with ships. Apparently in certain sections the mud literally bristles with old pins, surely drawn together by the tides. Once used in vast numbers for holding together everyday items, their modern equivalent is probably the dreaded material we cannot escape that is strangling our planet to death. Plastic. As for the pins, they might once have held together dresses, baby swaddles, shrouds.

My mother no longer walks along the river. She has incurable breast cancer and these days only leaves home to attend hospital appointments. We had only recently learnt that her treatment was no longer working. The news was still rippling out across our family. The realisation that the time we always knew was going to run out was running out faster. That day, the day of my sister's birthday, my mother, father and sister went down to the small stretch of the riverbank opposite their flat, reached by a green we have always called the little park. My mother produced some wildflower seeds out of the folds of her sari, from where many green things have appeared over the years. Cuttings, randomly picked flowers and, only in India, jasmine to be tucked roughly into our hair. The three of them sprinkled the seeds along the muddy towpath. Some words were spoken about our children, their grandchildren, seeing the wildflowers in the future. When my sister recounted this story to me on the phone we got upset and the words were stolen from our mouths, so what I know about this walk is sparse. I know neither what the flowers are nor where the seeds were scattered. What I know is this. I will keep crossing between Scotland and England. I will keep walking those paths. And the Thames mud will continue to hold history in its miry depths.

Lunar Cycling

LINDA CRACKNELL

My desk: a scatter of books, maps, letters, pebbles, and amongst them a relic which recalls me to another place, another daily pattern, another way of counting time. Mundane, yet treasured, this pedal from a child's bicycle is made of moulded creamy-white plastic and trimmed with two intact strips of reflector. I'll never know how it separated from its crank and chain and frame and wheels, or where it came from or whose foot once pressed it.

What's left of the spindle is rusty and encrusted with so-called acorn barnacles. They also cluster on its surfaces: on one side sparse and tiny as punctuation marks; on the other, swarming in a small colony and anchored into crevices between the treads. I know now that they once swam in a throng of delicate cyprid larvae, until they dropped from the sea's surface with a finite time to find a trustworthy home. Head down, appendages or leg-like 'cirri' up, they landed on the pedal and cemented them-selves to it, each growing six shell-plates around a vulnerable head, gills and legs, whilst at the top, four flat plates made a diamond-shaped 'door' to open and close with the tides.

This transformation, one of several including six stages beforehand as nauplii larvae, is as audacious as the butterfly's emergence from a cocoon, although in the opposite direction – from free-moving to sessile. For the remainder of their lives, which can be up to eight years, these crustaceans would remain fixed to a human tool of travel and revolutions; passenger-barnacles who cycled through the tides.

I found the pedal in the summer of 2017 during a month's stay at the Cove Park Artists' Residency on the Rosneath peninsula. Low-lying, with a higher spine of snarly moor and plantation forest, the peninsula dangles south into the Clyde with Loch Long to its west, bringing the wild to snag against the lawns of Victorian mansions at Cove. The waters of Gare Loch to the east bump up to caravans at Castle Point where holidaymakers from Glasgow swell the population each summer. Attached to Arrochar and its craggy 'Alps' only by a narrow isthmus, it was easy on this leg of land to imagine myself cut off. Once there, I designated as my fourth, northern, shore the road running coast to coast from Coulport, and committed myself to 'island' life.

I knew I'd need daily exercise, an escape from my desk, and that a new landscape would compel me to explore, so I decided to walk the entire coastline, tackling each section at the lowest point of the tide. Being there for twenty-eight days, I'd witness a complete lunar cycle: two neap tides, when the difference between high and low water is smallest, and two spring tides around the full and new moon, when it is greatest.

With a tidal cycle taking roughly twelve and a half hours, I left my desk at a different time each day, gradually progressing from morning to evening. My days were regulated, but in a way, irregular: my low-tide walks an unbreakable daily appointment offering a cosmic discipline and a stroll with a sense of purpose. 'Ardpeaton for the 9.52', I recorded in my notebook on day eleven, as if I was catching a bus. The next day, I caught the 10.41.

Using my bicycle (pedals still attached), I circled the twelve-mile loop of road to a different coastal point each day, finding rocky shores, occasional mudflats, little bays of sand and shingle, leggy jetties. In this way, I learnt the place through its shoreline, with its pillboxes, fishermen, mussel beds.

Where deciduous woodland met the coast around Rosneath Bay, the canopy had been salt-pruned by spring tides so that during the ebb, foliage hung to a sharp horizontal line well above the shore. High tides had also quarried soil away leaving tree roots cage-like, proud of the bank, reminiscent of mangroves. Occasionally I passed CCTV cameras, signs for Neighbourhood Watch, and experienced a shiver of surveillance. Walking around Rosneath Point one evening beside uneasy, clattery woodlands, I passed a fire which had been left raging and unsupervised on a boulder whilst curlews and oyster-catchers called and seals howled from Perch Rock.

Although the range between high and low tide is moderate here, a significant space opened up when the sea withdrew. My explorations developed a pattern. First I crossed the wet 'intertidal zone' to reach the water's edge, sometimes over rock slippery with bladderwrack. Watching for waterborne birds or vessels, I'd feel the wind direction, notice how a change in weather often accompanied the pendulum swing of the tide. Then I'd step along the wet space, teeming with visible and invisible lives following their interwoven biologies. Tidal pools captured a marine microcosm of fixed creatures or slow-movers, encrustations, vivid colours, the dance of light and water, things that waft: a lavish chest spilling treasure that had nothing to do with me.

I also observed the strandline where the spring tides leave their gifts. It's not uncommon for gunshot cartridges from Newfoundland to be washed up on Scotland's west coast as well as 'drift seeds' from tropical waters, in folk custom marvellous enough to hang as a charm around a neck and be called 'puzzle-fruit', or to find soil and grow into something exotic.

On each walk I took photos, made sound recordings, scribbled about sensory observations. Alongside rafts of eider on Loch Long, I noted a flotilla of warships and tugs escorting a nuclear submarine out into deep water. It must have been one of the four Vanguard-class sub-marines based at Faslane on Gare Loch, skirting Rosneath to load Trident warheads at Royal Naval Armaments Depot (RNAD) Coulport, before setting off on a lengthy submerged patrol somewhere in the world.

At twice the length of a jumbo jet, the submarine riding the surface of Loch Long with its long vapour trail and fanfare-flotilla seemed both furtive and highly visible. Once I'd witnessed it, the peninsula between these two colonised Clyde lochs felt snarled in a Cold War past which has rallied peaceful protesters since the 1960s. Improbable developments, when you consider that Coulport was a holiday destination for Glasgow gentry and former home of the nineteenth-century Kibble Palace glasshouse now erected in Glasgow's Botanic Gardens.

A police boat always lurked offshore as I wandered, its angled bow suggesting targeted binoculars. Inevitably one day it brought a friendly police officer in a car to enquire why I was walking towards the sentried razor-wire fence defending RNAD Coulport – razor-wire which, as I pointed out, would be totally ineffective at low tide when I could simply walk around it.

Without having planned to, I began to gather a few objects on each walk. Initially I homed in on those that pleased aesthetically: pebbles or pearly-lined shells, tea-cup or mug handles, coloured glass scoured to a dull beauty, and chinks of blue and white china once so cheap it was used as ship ballast. Perhaps these were beachcombing clichés. Although I also photographed a dead rock goby, a jellyfish with its rosette of minute red compass grada-tions, rocks draped with Trump-like hair, I mostly collected human-made things: train tickets, a doll's head, fishing floats, a blue plastic fisherman's glove separated for ever from its (g)love-lorn partner.

Different stretches of the coast offered different human debris. Apart from the ubiquitous tampon applicators and bottle lids, there was less plastic on the inland reaches of Loch Long than on the eastern shore close to the caravan park, where Helensburgh glittered across the water. Domestic ceramics from garden pots to porcelain lay in fragments close to the villages. Red bricks from Accrington. Tiles were the currency on Portkil Point near the village of Kilcreggan, along with the wrecks of 'leadless glazed' toilet bowls from Shanks and Co Ltd in Barrhead, a company world-renowned in the nineteenth and early twentieth centuries for innovations in plumbing and sanitation. But it was entanglements of the natural with the manufactured which increasingly became my collecting focus.

We seem to have no adequate common word for the place uncovered at low tide: the 'littoral' is slippery in our understanding. A place that isn't always there, reeking of repellent odours. Ungainly on two legs, we don't seem to belong, whereas wading birds, molluscs, crustaceans and specialised plants know how to live there. Yet this place of continuous renewal is an important source of food in many human cultures. Edible shellfish gathered here were once known in Orkney as 'ebb meat'.

When the shore is sandy, gradually sloping so that the waters retreat a great distance, most lifeforms are buried under the sand and it appears barren. It invites us to walk out onto a shiny no-man's-land that lays another sky beneath our feet. Here we might fall through into a different world or a seal adopt a human form. This space between two identifiable states has fostered a long-standing belief that no one can own it.

Our contemporary human lives march in circadian rhythms, according to dark and light, the twelve-hour, twenty-four-hour clock. Perhaps tidal rhythms seem irrelevant unless we are bait-diggers, shellfish-pickers, seafarers dependent on certain states of sea to leave or return to a port. Or perhaps we believe we can outsmart cosmic forces.

In coastal communities it used to be thought that death could only come during the ebb. Survive the turn to flood, and all was well, at least for the next twelve hours or so. Tides bring us the solace of reliable change. During my Rosneath stay I'd often find myself cycling breathlessly on one of the upper lanes at the time of high tide, exhilarated by Arran's serrated skyline and the red-and-white-liveried ferries plying between Gourock and Dunoon. High tide seemed to trigger high energy, whereas intuitively I found the ebb melancholic: a time for wandering and pondering.

Tide times are predictable; the tables are published long in advance. That our ancestors found them orderly is summed up by our word 'tidy', indicating 'things as they should be'. And the intertidal zone itself is characterised by everything being in its place; disciplined bands for different kinds of life, all observing the tides in their own rhythms. Barnacle settlements point to the limit of the 'upper shore' as defined biologically, leaving anything higher up to lichens and periwinkles, the most tolerant to drying out.

In Scotland we never live more than sixty or so miles from the coast, yet find tides mysterious. As humans we are 60 per cent water, our female reproduction cycles relate in some half-remembered way to lunar ones, and even our behaviour is understood by medical experts to be affected by the full moon.

Sensitised to these cycles myself during that month, I noticed poor sleep a few days either side of the full moon, felt an onrush of creative energy as the new moon began to swell. I've long been obsessed by weather forecasts when travelling to different parts of the country, but since then, if the place is coastal, I've also established the state of moon and tide. The flicker of a buried pulse in me makes me wonder: despite the decline of the moon's magnetism, might we still harbour responses to lunar and tidal cycles in our bodies as periwinkles apparently do even when removed to a lab?

Peaton Layo is a curved spit of land stretching from a shallow stony beach into Loch Long. From my cabin I dropped steeply on a hawthorn-hedged path to cross the Coulport Road, wading through a field of meadow flowers to arrive at a changed flora breaking through shingle: clumps of white sea campion – known in Gaelic as the 'little sea cauldron' for the shape of its sepal tube – fleshy stonecrop, sea plantain, sea asters.

From the spit, a small bay scooped away either side of me, each ringed with parallel lines of deep-red seaweed archiving the various heights of the tide. It was here on day sixteen, midway between a neap and spring tide, that I found the barnacled bicycle pedal cast up high and dry. It seized me with its visual quip on the contrary pulls of settling and travelling, although in maintaining a roaming life, perhaps these cycling-barnacles made a bad choice. But it also spoke of nature's way of using what we discard; how our relics might be colonised once the Anthropocene is over.

I'd noticed barnacles coating every solid surface around the shoreline. They scraped my hands as I scrambled on exposed south-westerly-facing rocks, where their cone-shape keeps them resilient to surf-lashings. They have long been regarded as a nuisance for 'fouling' the sleek hulls of boats and thus slowing them, or clogging up engine intakes or exhausts. They may be chiselled off. An industry has been made out of poisons to stop them settling. Yet the infamous power of the barnacles' lifetime cement means another industry has emulated its qualities for glue manufacture.

Their colonies spread a distinctive patina on rocks which, imagined on a different scale, suggest antique lands, each volcano uniquely patterned with converging ridges and gullies. Close up, they resemble a field of old men's tobacco-stained molars. So abundant, so immovable, so still, we may think of them as stone.

But a wet, barnacle-gnarly rock stopped me one evening as I wandered an emptied-out Culwatty Bay. Reflected sunlight pulsed all over its surface. Under a magnifying glass I saw through the film of water the shells' diamond-shaped hatches opening and closing, their hair-delicate 'legs' wafting together in a net to catch plankton. The sight thrilled me: a privileged insight into a small, pulsing life previously invisible. Rather than inanimate, the barnacles came alive in my mind and were, literally, kicking. If and when the rock dried out, the shells would close, trapping aerated water around their gills, allowing the creatures to sit out a period of even considerable heat until the tide turned. Hard-wired into them are rhythms of immersion and drying-out; their feeding and breathing is determined by the gravitational pull of sun and moon, revolutions of the moon around earth and the alignment of both with the sun.

Semibalanus balanoides, these most widespread of barnacles, depend on a low mean sea temperature for breeding. With warming seas now, I wonder if they will move northwards as part of the current mass relocation of species. Marine life is said to be moving four times faster than the land-based. Estimates vary, but Britain's coastline, fractured by unique collaborations of tide and geology, is as much as 20,000 miles long with the main islands included. I picture the barnacles industriously tracing every rocky inlet and craggy peninsula, encircling us within a fortified wall. It's a familiar and disregarded feature of our salted sometimes-shores. My month of observing tidal patterns, treading places defined by the reciprocity of land and sea, taught me to treasure it. And my relic-paperweight helps me to remember.

Plastic Megaliths

HAYDEN LORIMER

I love portals into the past. There's one in particular I
keep turning to. Slipping through alone, sometimes
in company. It's in rural Aberdeenshire, set back a little
from the life of the nearby village, over the road from a
cul-de-sac of red brick bungalows and beech hedges, just
beyond the community recycling point. A tree-fringed
vale: no larger than a field in these parts. I pay my visits
around the wheel of the year. When it's dusted by snow,
freshly in bud, during full and fallen leaf. The place keeps
its own secret: the remains of a modern ruin. A perfect
spot for mooning about in, and seeing how stuff stands
up to the test of time.

Archaeolink first opened as a visitor attraction during
the previous millennium. The clue was there in the name:
it was intended as a bridging point between worlds past
and present, in the heart of a regional landscape notable
for its rich concentration of surviving prehistoric sites.
It boasted multiple attractions: a facsimile of a recumbent
stone circle, a pair of impressive replica roundhouses, a

farmstead, a military encampment and a wickerman, standing forty feet high, built of willow-bundles, set alight following an annual torchlight procession to mark *Samhain*, the ancient Celtic harvest festival. 'Leaves of Time', a prehistoric tree trail, led the more adventurous on a steady rise of zigzags, planted with hazel, ash, alder, holly, blackthorn, elder, rowan, oak and bird cherry. The ascent crested on the flattened top of Berryhill where the reward for effort lay beneath your feet: the foundation stones of an ancient hill fort (real rather than artificial). Today, the foot traffic has gone, save for the occasional dog-walker, but the arboretum continues to prosper entirely of its own accord.

Dreamt up by local councillors, Archaeolink was a modern heritage concept made real. It was endorsed by the regional business development agency, and turbocharged by a grant from the European Union's 'Leader Community Initiative'. In 1997, it was a boom-time for Britain's can-do cultural sector, framed by a greater political vision about how things were only getting better. The ribbon-cutter at the launch event was Sir Tony Robinson, celebrity presenter of *Time Team*, a show devoted to archaeological investigations, and a political activist who was soon to be elected to the Labour Party's National Executive Committee. At the spot where he posed, hamming it up for the press pack's photographers, things are slowly deliquescing. Archaeolink shut up shop in 2011. Now weeds sprout from the base of the interpretation panel that once bid a welcome, partially obscuring the EU flag with its circle of bright yellow stars studded on a blue field. It's a melancholic marker for an era of infrastructural investment and a longer spiral of decline.

All about, new growth consumes what once was carefully clean cut. Grasses lengthen. Tussocks thicken. Gorse creeps over and around the curving earthworks, crowding out the raised walkways. The ferns and bracken rise high enough to brush at my passing shoulder. Come midsummer, nettles and thistles make *ruinenlust* a long-trousered and long-sleeved affair. It's a case of skirting, squeezing and tiptoeing, each quest slower and more circuitous than the last. The flowering planters once lining the entranceway have split at the seams. Barrel struts splay like petals, spongy green innards spilling and disgorging groundward.

If the modern heritage movement has a prevailing philosophy, it's that the passing of time and the nature of change are phenomena in need of curating and stage-managing. In return for the entrance fee, visitors to Archaeolink were given a sense of time passing through the life of one place, its peoples and their cultural practices, across the earliest periods of human history. Would-be time-travellers began their tour in the Neolithic period, journeyed through the Bronze Age, then the Iron Age, before calling it a day after the Romans' arrival in the time of the Picts. For heritage industry insiders *au fait* with the terminology of the experience economy,

Archaeolink was 'a destination'. Not a theme park, but a park where prehistory was the theme for exploration and education. As an entry-point to antiquarianism, it offered up the usual mix of educational events, theme days and family-centred fun. As well as push-button playthings, gadgetry and gimmicks, there were displays of living history. People were employed to demonstrate woodworking, coracle construction, hut-building (by the wattle and daub method), roof-thatching, hedge-laying, wool-dyeing (with fleece shorn from the ancient sheep breeds kept on site). Marked paths kept the tourists on track.

Culturally speaking, Archaeolink was positioned at a crossroads between the profound and the playful. Staff invited local schoolchildren to imagine a day far in the future when archaeologists would be attracted to excavate the site. The kids were tasked with readying a Y2K time capsule for burial at a ceremony on the eve of the new millennium. Its contents were to be an expression of contemporary youth culture. The Class of '99 chose a CD copy of *Spiceworld*, the Spice Girls' second album, a Pot Noodle (spicy chicken flavour), a pair of Nike sneakers, and that day's edition of the *Press & Journal*. To the best of anyone's knowledge the capsule remains undisturbed, submerged a few feet under.

When Grampian's gateway to the prehistoric snapped shut, a link to the past was broken. The media had their way with the story, in headlines at times a little cruelly cast. After fourteen years, Archaeolink had become a failed attraction. There were money troubles right from the start. Initial business plans projected more than 100,000 people passing through the turnstiles each year. Actual visitors only ever approached a tenth of the target. For every punter who paid their way, the council was reportedly contributing a subsidy of £13. With running costs spiralling – some put the annual deficit in excess of £100,000 – prehistory proved an unaffordable luxury. A call for alternative backers drew a blank. The property was deemed to have 'served its use as a tourist facility'. Putting it up for sale was judged 'the most sensible way forward'.

Years since going to market, the site still pops up on the council's online catalogue of saleable assets, amenities and real estate. The list features all manner of municipal cultural and entrepreneurial architecture deemed surplus to community requirements, mothballed to minimise the strain on the public purse, and up for grabs to any willing bidder. Public toilets, police stations, workshops, depots and stores, cemetery keeper's lodges, primary schools with adjoining master's lodgings, industrial units and business parks.

Archaeolink sticks out like a sore thumb. But in hard times, it's a buyer's market. And the strath is plastered with large roadside signs trumpeting other futures full of promise – 'PLOTS FOR SALE', 'PLANNING PERMISSION FOR ONE', 'UNIQUE DEVELOP-MENT OPPORTUNITY'. Affordable housing, I've read it reported, is at a premium in rural parts. The reasons are various. Second home purchases can swallow a village whole. Or break it in two. And holiday letting (by the explosively successful online BnB model) is the latest economic force to be reckoned with. A resurgent counterculture offers hope for the brave and the bold: self-building, going off-grid, downsizing, taking to the woods. Campaigners for 'A Thousand Huts' push the case for the countryside as a place to live simply and sustainably, where the prospect of owning a tiny home is more than mere #cabinporn. But the prospect of occupying a coarse reconstruction of an Iron Age roundhouse isn't to everyone's taste. Taking shelter in one during a thundery downpour, I had time to consider the options, going over practicalities, dreaming a different life. Beneath the heather-thatch, I felt the prick of something primal. Housing stock left lying idle signalled a connection with nameless forebears across the ages. Having somewhere safe and secure enough to settle ranks as one of our most basic human needs.

That substance and structure can so quickly go to seed ought to come as no great surprise. Archaeolink's design team avoided any clear distinction between architecture and landscaping. Instead, semi-subterranean buildings were formed from incisions made in the earth, and an ingeniously chiselled profile. The firm contracted for the job had a track record of working with prehistoric heritage, previously producing plans to improve public access to Stonehenge's ring of standing stones while treating the landscape of the Salisbury Plain with sensitivity. Even in its heyday, everything about Archaeolink was low-slung. The visitor centre's reinforced concrete slab roof was turfed over. Broad-paned glazing opened onto wide valley views, reflecting a rustic palette of brown, green and yellow back indoors. Earthen ramps, bunds and grassy embankments radiated out from a central tumulus housing indoor exhibition areas and an auditorium space. Peephole windows, allowing shafts of daylight into the darkness, were housed in concrete pipes that pierced the conical grass hill.

Critics of the day made appreciative noises about shapely references to domed burial mounds and the comforting sense of continuity created. Archaeolink even featured in a special centenary-year issue of *Country Life* celebrating contemporary British buildings of distinction. Others thought it looked like the set for *Teletubbies*.

The original scheme was for Archaeolink's hub and spoke design to work panoramically, along axes far beyond the site itself. And as a contemporary ruin, it still does, drawing the eye along sightlines to cardinal points in the surrounding landscape. The Hill of Dunnideer is principal among them. Five miles distant, pyramidal in form, though only modest in height, it is an outsized presence. Wherever you travel in the strath, Dunnideer appears. Sometimes it rears or funnels, elsewhere it pokes and peeps, but always it grounds. Its pull can feel magnetic. And for good reason, it would seem.

Five thousand years ago, the hill was deeply meaningful to the people who lived in the area. Theories about Neolithic cosmology are based on charting complex correspondences between the shape of the land and the astral map of the night sky. Stone circles were a topographic technology that enabled one to be read against the other, and surely rank as the greatest cultural achievement of the prehistoric period. All told, fifty-nine were built across the North East. A dozen of them were placed to align with a view of the Hill of Dunnideer. Archaeo-astronomers are in general agreement about explanations for the ring arrangement and individual positioning of the megaliths. The largest, lodged horizontally, and its two tall flankers, mounted vertically, were orientated towards the south-west, to form the frame for a sacred ceremony, occurring on one night only, when according to the sky calendar, worshippers would witness the passage of the moon as it skimmed the uppermost edge of the recumbent stone. These were circular earth temples with every reason to remain roofless.

Some speculators out on the ragged edge of archaeological theory even dare to suggest a lost mythos of landscape when the presiding deity was female: a great Goddess, made manifest in a magic mother mountain and sacred sister hills, realised in a matriarchal society, where life fell under the rule of proto she-punks. An ancient psychogeography of 'Girl Power' long before Posh, Ginger, Baby, Scary and Sporty were stars ascendant.

On top of Berryhill, where the Archaeolink tree-trail peters out and no interpretation panel survives, it's a worldview that seems far from fanciful. From there you can see the lattice of lanes and homesteads, then the pine-skirted lower slopes of Bennachie and, on high, a skyline of granite tors, carrying names in a natal language that speaks of protective and nurturing associations rooted in place. Oxen Craig, Mither Tap, Maiden Pap. Watch Craig.

With school out for the Easter break, and the forecast set fair, my son felt ready to indulge another bout of ruin bothering at Archaeolink. There's enough of the noir in it to tempt an early teen outdoors. We drifted about the site, searching for unexplored corners.

'Dad!' came the shout.

And again, louder this time, more insistent, his glee barely suppressed:

'*Dad!* It's OPEN!'"

The look on his face told me everything I needed to know. That this was what counted as father-and-son archaeology. All of a sudden our jaunt developed a different dimension. Slithering to the bottom of the grass slope we hovered over the threshold of the visitor centre, inspecting where the padlock and steel hasp had been prized away from the protective chipboard sheeting. At our feet, cubes of shattered glass glinted in the morning light. A peacock butterfly sat open-winged, decorations on full display. The whole scene looked artfully staged, as if to raise awkward questions about our purpose and intent. My concerns were about poor parenting, and the prospect of a bungling outlaw duo getting lifted by the polis for breaking and entering. And how Good Friday seemed the very worst date to be found behaving badly. His anxieties were more vivid. Upon entering the sunken chamber were we likely to trigger some Pictish equivalent of the Pharaoh's Curse . . . ?

Inside the bunker, the chill of concrete was unmistakable. We inched forward. A mildewed creep, all the better to pick through what had already been ransacked. Archaeolink's administrative midden was laid bare: technical reports, audit responses, policy briefings, funding applications, subject curricula. Soiled gift-shop stock: postcards, till rolls, chunky wooden jigsaw puzzle pieces forming runic symbols, a stack of Roman centurions' shields. We indulged in the kind of goofing that conditions of abandonment seem always to invite: deceptive feats of superhuman strength with hollow plastic megaliths; the cut-and-thrust of a mock sword fight ('Take that! And that! Aaaand *that*!'); the inevitable snaps for the photo roll ('Hey, get one of me inside the coracle!').

Using a smartphone torch to guide us on our way, we edged into darkened exhibition areas, directing the beam to cast light on tiny set-piece tableaux, recessed into the walls. Shadowy figures appeared, moving about the land, silhouetted against its relief. They were getting on with things, as far as we could see: building, hunting, skinning, cooking, eating, tending. Quietly coming into being, untroubled by thoughts of what they might yet want to do with their lives.

From whose point of view is prehistoric life to be told? We might sketch the outlines of their existence, the bare bones of the story. But we struggle to inhabit the prehistoric mind, to ascertain their sense of the human spirit. We know precious little of their social affairs and bonds of community: the plays of power, the dynamics and dramas of family life, their values and systems of belief, their need for ritual and performance, even the most general codes for normal interaction. Their interior worlds – worries and fears, hopes and dreams – remain a mystery. By their weapons we can grasp certain brutal truths. We see the scars left by acts of violence, or from waging war, and wonder at their swirling chaos. What we know of their elaborate culture of death delights and discomfits in equal measure. By their tools we know their craft and their skills, and the artistry of their material forms. We have hints at what gave them aesthetic pleasure, but through a system of symbols that we must guess at, in a code we are struggling to crack. And so we continue to pace the circumference of their stone circles searching for a consoling sign.

It's akin to a view of their world through a pinhole camera. Or the darkness of a diorama only dimly illuminated by a phone whose battery charge is fading fast. Predictably enough, our talk turned to trophy hunting, and how one item might just about be acceptable. Something pocket-sized, we agreed. His pick: a miniature model of an animal hide stretched taut on a drying rack. Trove taken, we blinked our way back out into spring sunshine, letting the portal close, and leaving prehistory to the weeds.

Signs for Alva

DAVID JAMES GRINLY

Littoral Rising

GERRY LOOSE

I

AFTER AMERGIN

am glacier rolling back
am tsunami
am beaching whale
am the bones of every curlew
am stag starving on hill
am hawk down to bone
am wilt of green plant
am ribcage hind
am salmon infested with lice
am the end of words
am burning teardrop
am salt ocean in woodland
am plastic in every pore
am head burst with fire

who gouges & grubs blue mountains
who trudges the crescent moon
who stores suns in buried bunkers
who leaches the fecund topsoils
whose alibi is god
who stands at the edge
who holds back the typhoon

2

Thalassa Thalassa
how littoral slides into us
edge become centre

coffin sea-road
a gesture of longshore drift
of foreshore & nearshore

how the oceans rise in them
& they clamp shells to ears
to contain surf

sweet sap rises in them
to restrain salt from eyes

barnacles & men of war
in upper branches
their canopies bird wings

the strand become charnel
the eyes' restless waves

deep tribes of swimfish
as architecture of water

nippled porpoises
as sea-surge of wheatfield

that slow mountain wave
that slow mountain swimming

& how sky holds up the waters
& the oceans roost in trees

& islands disappear
in salt

3

AFTER PSALM 74

Oh man, why does your anger burn with acrid
  smoke?
Why do your tramplings deliver perpetual desolations?
How should you be rewarded for clear-felling each
  ancient forest?
What is the price of breaking the five wild oceans?
What are your terrible secrets spoken in the mouth of
  Leviathan?
Where now is the stolen soul of the turtle dove?
Oh man, stand up: plead your own cause.

4

after nothing
as lines are drawn

for the sea
so for the coast

as docken rusts
so the burnet rose

stem by stem purple
foxgloves reach higher

yellow mustard
& yellow crusts of lichen

singing pink thrift
woodbine surging

pignut & cow parsley
drift on drift in June sun

whitecaps of elder froth
winged rust of sycamore seed

so are we
it is

as grace loaned

A Handful of Talons

JIM CRUMLEY

H ere is a question you will never have been asked before: how close have you been to the talons of a sea eagle? I have two reasons for asking.

The first is that if you have ever seen a sea eagle (and depending on whether it was flying or perched), the chances are that you were impressed by its wingspan or its beak. I choose to presume evolution knew what it was doing when it signed off on the final design of these components (if it *is* the final design, for with evolution who knows?), but my inexpert eye has always thought the designers exceeded what was strictly necessary to get the job done in pursuit of ostentation. In any case, talons are unlikely to have crossed your mind.

The second reason is that if you were to ask me the same question, I would answer that I have had four sea eagle talons in the palm of my left hand, and that the moment remains one of the most enduring of my nature writing life. It should be said that there was no sea eagle attached to the talons at the time, and that (give or take a hundred years) they were five thousand years old.

I had just begun working on a book called *The Eagle's Way* (Saraband, 2014). I had become intrigued by the increasing impact of sea eagles in some of my preferred landscapes following an east coast reintroduction project near the Firth of Tay between 2007 and 2012. A breeding population had already consolidated in the Hebrides and the West Highlands, and especially around Mull and Skye, following reintroductions in the last quarter of the twentieth century. Young sea eagles are great wanderers, but now some of the east coast birds had begun to fly right across the country on a single line of latitude from the Firth of Tay to Mull. Then I heard about three east coast birds roosting in a pinewood above Loch Tay. When I investigated I discovered that a young golden eagle was tagging along, apparently for company, and I could find no one who had heard of such behaviour before. And while the sea eagles had come from the east, the golden eagle almost certainly came from the west. I began to wonder if a two-way, coast-to-coast eagle highway was being opened up by wandering young birds widening their horizons. In the years since then, that theory has borne some persuasive fruit. But what really fascinated me was whether this behaviour was utterly new, or was it very old indeed and had it begun to reoccur only because the new circumstances offered by the east coast reintroduction had made it possible?

A second aspect of sea eagle behaviour had already become self-evident in Scotland: this is a bird that is unafraid to come in among us. It does not share the golden eagle's intolerance of human company, and sometimes appears to seek it out. And if that is true now, was it always true? I went to Orkney in search of answers, to Isbister on South Ronaldsay, for there lies the Tomb of the Eagles, a Neolithic chambered burial cairn with a unique story to tell, a story about how, 5,000 years ago, people and sea eagles learned to live – and die – together.

The Tomb of the Eagles was discovered in 1958 by Ronnie Simison, a local farmer, who noticed that a grassy mound a few yards from sea cliffs had begun to erode, revealing horizontally laid stones. His curiosity was roused. What would emerge in time was a burial tomb that accommodated 16,000 human bones, the remains of over 300 people, and – remarkably – the bones and skulls and talons of sea eagles. The eagles had been interred alongside the people. *Tomb of the Eagles*, the definitive book about the site by archaeologist John W. Hedges, has an apt subtitle, *A Window on Stone Age Britain*. For what had been discovered was effectively a tribal burial ground, a tribe for whom the sea eagle had some kind of totemic significance. Carbon-dating of the bones has shown that the burial ground was in use for 800 years.

Twentieth and twenty-first century restoration means that now you and I can crawl inside (or haul yourself along with an ingenious rope-and-trolley arrangement designed by Ronnie Simison) and emerge at the end of the tomb's entrance passage into an exquisite showpiece of Neolithic architecture. There is also a state-of-the-art visitor centre, which is both a lasting tribute to the lives of Ronnie and his wife Morgan and a fitting home for the tomb's artefacts. It was there, in the visitor centre, five thousand years after the tomb's heyday, that a woman with an Orkney voice which undulated in sea cadences like waves, extended her hand towards me and said, 'Here, hold them', and pressed four five-thousand-year-old sea eagle talons into the palm of my left hand. Instinctively I cupped my hand so that they huddled together. Like eggs in a nest, I thought.

My next thought was this:

These talons flew.

My mind's eye reattached them to the bird on which they had grown, on which they grabbed fish, duck, gannet, goose, swan, cormorant, curlew, lamb (stillborn, weak, careless or carelessly tended by ewe or shepherd), newborn deer maybe, and then they choked or crushed or bled the life out of them.

Those same talons left imprints in snow and sand and low-tide mud, *five thousand years ago*. They gave off a presence, like a scent, a blended incense of the eerie and the intimate. They were yellowed and blunted by the passage of so much time since they performed any function at all. I was astounded by their survival, baffled by what to make of the moment, for it had no reference points in my life at all.

I have seen sea eagle talons at work, watched them lift an eider duck from the surface of Talisker Bay on Skye, for example. A group of four eiders dived as the eagle flew over, the eagle waited, circling – small, tight circles – then glided down with wings wide, feet lowered, reaching the surface at precisely the same instant and in precisely the same place as one of the drakes surfaced. The legs reached forward then snapped back, the talons bit. The eider cleared the surface of the water, wings thrashing. Eagle wings powered its last flight.

Likewise, I have heard about a mid-air attack on a mute swan. Golden eagles take geese in mid-air and sea eagles are bigger, heavier, more powerful. Bringing down a swan is ambitious but not out of the question. I have seen the sea eagle's deeply incised footprints in tidal mud on Mull, in damp sand at Tentsmuir Point, North Fife, where the waters of the Tay and the North Sea comingle. I have seen sea eagles in coastal communities from Port Ramsay on Lismore to Lochaline and Glenelg in the mainland west, to Auchmithie and Tayport in the mainland east; and in Highland heartlands like Loch Tay and Loch Tulla and Abernethy Forest. Unlike golden eagles, they leave a lot of footprints in places where people leave theirs. That's when you notice the talons.

But these four talons in the cupped palm of my hand, so snug there they looked as if they might hatch . . . how could I be indifferent about the fate of the bird that wore them?

And consider this: these same talons almost certainly pierced human flesh, while the daffodil-shaded beak tore it open and swallowed it. For the truly astounding part of the story that the Tomb of the Eagles has to tell is that the bones of the people and the bones – and the talons – of the sea eagles were reverentially buried alongside each other, in acknowledgement of the unique service the eagles had provided for the people for eight hundred years, and which was nothing less than the purification of human corpses before interment. We call it 'sky burial' now, for it still happens in far-flung airts (Nepal is one such). The corpse is laid out on a raised stretcher, and before it is buried or otherwise sanctified, its flesh is stripped from its bones by raptors, mostly eagles, purifying the life that was lived. But what is unique about Orkney is that the purifiers themselves, the corpse-eaters, the sea eagles, were so honoured.

The tomb lies a mile from the visitor centre. You can see it in the distance, and in truth it looks like nothing at all: a low grassy hump. I walked the path on a May morning anthemed by skylarks and curlews, every step landed among ground-hugging, wind-cheating flowers – eyebright, primrose, spring squill, marsh orchid, gorgeous grass of Parnassus. Oystercatchers and lapwings added a run-the-gauntlet spice to the walk. An arctic skua, a beautifully lethal missile of a bird, scorched across the fields with six lapwings in raucous pursuit.

Then the shining sea, gannets. Then the tomb, a low green rise on a quiet shelf just yards from low cliffs, a wide flagstone 'courtyard'. For a few moments, I was really not in the mood for a burial cairn. Then I hauled myself in, and it was some time before I was in the mood to leave.

The Isbister tomb was not a one-off. There are seventy-six such tombs in Orkney. Some of the others are shared with animal bones: perhaps different tribes with different tribal totems. Archaeologically speaking, Isbister is just the pick of the bunch, and I might say the same from the point of view of a nature writer with a love of eagles.

But here's a thing: months after I held the talons, the feeling of their feather-lightness in my left palm would recur unpredictably, as if they were still there: invisible talisman, inaudible summons. Every time, I would cup my hand in response to the sensation and my mind hurtled back to Isbister, to the bright, larksong-drenched headland, the cool, grey, flat-stone inscape of the tomb, the sea-shaded voice of the woman who reached a hand towards me and said, 'Here, hold them.'

A life like mine turns on such moments. I began to think of the sea eagle as a kind of ambassador, painstakingly schooled in the task of advancing nature's cause.

Shortly after my visit, a journal called *Bird Study* issued a report about the relative populations of golden eagles and sea eagles in Great Britain and Ireland through the last 5,000 years. Its population estimates showed that persecution was not a new phenomenon; rather it had been going on since around 500 AD. Yet what intrigued me more was that it included estimates from 3,000 BC, which is when the Isbister tomb was in operation and eagles were abundant enough to make possible the relationship between the many generations of the tomb builders and the birds. The relatively swift decline of the sea eagle reflects its willingness to live close to people, that and the fact that it is a slower, larger flier, an easier target. The golden eagle was never wiped out, never had to be reintroduced.

The numbers refer to breeding pairs:

Date	Golden Eagle	Sea Eagle
3,000 BC	650	2,550
500 AD	1,000–1,500	800–1,400
1800 AD	300–500	150
1920	100–200	Nil
1950	280	Nil
1971	400	Nil
2003	440	31

What changed? How did sea eagles get from 2,550 to nil? Our species lost its way. Slowly we forgot that we too were nature; we civilised, we industrialised, we settled and farmed and built and cleared from our path all those species that were suddenly inconvenient. The Victorians took all of that to new extremes and effected genocides against nature. The recovery from that nadir has been laborious.

That original reintroduction of the sea eagle into Scotland began on Rum in 1975 and the final five-year reintroduction project – on the south shore of the Firth of Tay – was completed in 2012. In the first twenty years of this century, the golden eagle population has eased gently upwards to just over 500 pairs, but over the same period the sea eagle population has soared – 106 pairs in 2015, but a Scottish Natural Heritage report of 2016 predicted that by 2040, 900 pairs is possible. It is, then, a matter of time before the sea eagle begins to outnumber the golden eagle again, an event that will signal a return to the historical norm. And while our own twenty-first century sensibilities are unlikely ever to indulge a return to the rituals of sky burial and the Isbister tomb, sooner rather than later our species must come to terms once again with the idea of living with eagles in our midst.

Most of us have never seen a golden eagle. Those of us who are familiar with it know it for a haunter of the high and lonely places, a specialist. It eats meat – other birds, mammals up to the size of a red deer calf, carrion. The sea eagle can do the high and lonely thing too, but it is a generalist both in its nesting and eating habits. It will eat almost anything, and if your house is convenient enough it will happily perch on your roof. The golden eagle is having to learn to live with it already but, unlike ourselves, it has not forgotten how. It is taking us a little longer to re-learn how to be a good neighbour to a sea eagle. Yet that visionary first step on Rum has proved to be both a turning point for nature in Scotland and a turning point for our relationship with nature, a sensational *mea culpa* for the crimes of our forefathers. And after Rum, an introduction project on the West Highland mainland consolidated the bird's presence along much of the western seaboard, whence it has found its own way inland, often to historic sea eagle nesting sites. Most of the old sites had not become unsuitable in the dark years simply because the birds were absent. And when I consider that idea, I consider Loch Tulla.

If you travel into the Highlands from the south through the gentler mountains of, say, Balquhidder or Loch Lomond, it is the unbroken sweep of Ben Dorain above Bridge of Orchy that signals your entry into heartland Highlands. Golden eagles still frequent conspicuous rocks called *Creag na h-Iolaire,* Eagle Crag. They are crags, buttresses and other outcrops, and they were named centuries ago, perhaps because from a particular community a particular rock looked like an eagle, but more often because eagles nested there or often perched or roosted there. A nest rock needs the right kind of ledge, often overhung, often shaded from direct sunlight for much of the day; a perching rock will usually have a wide view over a nesting territory. Some are an arduous day's march from the nearest road, but I know three you can watch from the road. They are rarely higher than about 1,500 feet, and some Hebridean ones are as near to sea level as makes very little difference. And many a sea eagle, whether embedded in the resurgent strongholds of the island west or wandering that way along their reinvented highway from the east, will recognise those rocks for what they are, and be intrigued by them because, in eagle eyes, they are the most coveted of places, as they were long before the landscape was named.

Historic sea eagle eyries have been identified hereabouts on islands in lochs, and Loch Tulla is one of these. So I invited myself on a fool's errand to see if I could track the spoor of the sea eagle on the edge of Rannoch Moor more than a hundred years after it was compulsorily evicted. But I had a straw to clutch: once an eagle rock, always an eagle rock. Or in this case, an eagle tree. Besides, long experience of this kind of escapade has taught me that a willingness to linger in the landscape I'm writing about usually pays off. So I turned off the main road beneath Ben Dorain at Bridge of Orchy for the single-track road to Loch Tulla, stepped from the car into boots, jacket, gloves and pinewood; at once, nature was a more demanding presence.

A short distance along the loch's pinewood shore was the tiny island that once accommodated a sea eagle nest. It is not hard to identify. It is the only island in the loch. And it still has trees, of a kind. The stony ground and the onslaughts of pretty well every wind that ever blew have restricted and twisted the ambitions of four larch trees that could be of almost any age at all. The solitary pine which keeps them company is dead straight and slim and surely a young tree. Welcome to Eilean an Stalcair, the Stalker's Island. I wonder if it is the smallest island in the land that has a name. And once upon a time, it had a sea eagle's nest, a thing of such monstrous dimensions that it looked as if it might capsize the whole island. Any day now, such a nest might once again transform the island's modest profile. The grapevine that whispers through these places has already brought word that a sea eagle paused here in the spring of 2010. It did not linger but it was here, and now of course it knows the way.

The very thought produces a strange feeling in the palm of my left hand.

I Da Welk Ebb

JEN HADFIELD

At first I think the lean, white mare is dead, lying on her back in a muddy paddock, a pair of *shalder* – oystercatchers – drilling unconcerned in the dried-up quagmire. I pull into the layby to see if the horse is still breathing. She sighs, grinding the two halves of her clam-like mouth, reassembling herself in a swing and judder of bony limbs, is suddenly upright. She reaches forward with a hind hoof to kick an itch on her face. When she shudders, a cloud of fine dust swells around her. We might not see a day this warm again all summer, hot enough to burn a sun-starved northern nose; wintry showers are forecast later in the week.

After equinoctial storms that I hope have excavated shellfish from their muddy beds, the day's freakishly still and the sky unclouded. Everything shimmers: the sea popping light like a glitterball. *Rare* is the only way I can think to describe the sea – as a pearl or jewel are described as rare. Its colour is a fine, pale mother-of-pearl enclosing Foula, the sheltered voes more like brushed metal; from the top of the hill it's the archetypal, imaginary island, lost in a shift of white haze so it seems to hover, as imaginary islands should.

In fact I think turning real places into imaginary ones is a dangerous practice. We do home harm when we let it be cast as an archipelago on the brink of fantasy. External projections upon real islands tend to exploit and misunderstand them, a Northern version of Orientalism – 'Borealism', perhaps – but even I find myself doing it sometimes. I've never been to Foula – its iceberg profile has hovered on my horizon, approaching and retreating in a dance of high and low pressure, appearing and disappearing, for twelve years now – and I have somehow chosen to keep it that way. Visible, but just out of reach. A container – a lamp – to fill with imaginary genies. Why do we need islands as repositories for our yearnings, when reality is so much more complex and delicious?

They say Shetlanders don't so much park as abandon their vehicles. I throw the car into the corner of a turning circle at the end of the Houlland road, and grab the daysack to strike out across the bog, startling up lapwings and, perhaps, a whimbrel. I'm hoping for thick-shelled mussels gone feral from the nearby farm, full of little grey granular pearls; cockles, like valentines half-buried in the mud; *smislins* (soft-shelled clams) and – since their price has gone up to three pounds a kilo – welks, those glossy, lion-headed gastropods that are *Littorina littorea* in Latin, whose friendly name is the common periwinkle. I scramble downhill and over the bog, aware of the minutes ticking down to low tide. Despite the sun, the cold wind is giving me a terrible face-ache – as if revealing the death mask under my skin. The pillowy sphagnum is lush and red. My greedy strides stab deep, weeping wounds in it. A fierce rush of relief and joy.

And – the journey from desk-writer to gatherer is like the journey from solitariness to mating: a total absorption in the now. The forage is a place where I'm lost to myself, and we're happy, I think, when we can forget ourselves. I wonder how it happens. Perhaps in escaping the most modern parts of our brain, the most recent operating system, if you like, the cleverest, most wry, most self-conscious and worldly layer, the bit that allows us to think about thinking, to understand, as if from the outside, that we have a mind at all: when we escape that, we can yomp downhill through luscious sphagnum bog back into our lost heaven

– where the tide is wayyyy out. The shore of the little estuary where the bog drains into the sea through shallow mudflats, the low promontory and its holm, are hemmed with a tawny brocade of seaweed. With a prehistoric screech, a *heggri* takes laborious flight. I stuff my gloved hands into long black fishgutter's gauntlets and pick my way into the water. Even through wellies and two pairs of socks, in thermal leggings and boilersuit, the sea is bloody cold, bone-crunchingly cold. I'm already half-planning to abandon my forage. But it's a nice place to be on a rare, still day. I flip quiffs of wrack on the rocks, looking for welks, peer through the muddling waves. The music hall 'oo-*oooh*!' of gossipy eiders skims across still water. I get a good view of the boys working the mussel farm, winching up ropes encrusted with valuable shellfish, and no doubt they get a good view of me too, stooping over the mudflats and rockpools. Then I spot a good bolus of fat welks just out of reach, and tiptoe hugely towards them through weed-hidden hollows. My boots slide. I get one foot caught between two rocks and teeter, almost losing my balance. The water's pressure creases my wellies, and puts the squeeze on them, until it finally overflows the cuffs. First trickle of the winter sea around my toes. I let my boots fill and the water steal the blood-warmth from my feet. In time it'll feel like a warm broth. I experience the first breach of a sequence of sea-safe hatches, leading to increasingly primal and neglected corridors, wending into the back rooms of the brain.

What happens in our brains when we forage? Why does it feel so good? I picked and picked with increasingly numb fingers, as the juicy weight of welks rolled against each other like sticky marbles in my swinging Co-op bag. My eye is keen, my greed measureless. What cold links are being cast in the forge of my cranium as I bend, guddle, glean, reach, ooze, moonwalk, probe, dell, *purl*

? – in the distance, cars are still streaming over the Burra Brig. Their rushy trill over the loose cattle-grid is audible, but somehow inconsequential. It's like gazing across at the Earth from the moon. Over there. But now, now.

138

The slack. Clear, tannin-rich water, the colour of *rooiboos* tea. A held breath. Now it feels like the flow of time has paused, and the water settles itself, becomes clear and still. The ocean – this is its hem, plumped meniscus like the eye's iris or the jellyfish's mantle – is poised, hushed. It occurs to me that what I'm standing in, what I'm wading through, is nothing less than the entire Atlantic, with the North Sea thrown into the bargain, and the Med through the cervix of the Gibraltar Strait and I'm shrinking

– now the transparent rooms I stand in are full and bustling with personae, and I move hesitantly and with infinite care through fragile rooms panelled in amber, in chartreuse-coloured breadcrumb sponge, like the chambers of a sea king: Charleroix Du Mer. The slippery kelps are laced with a fine brocade – sea mat or bryozoans, millions of cells, each tiny animal interdependent on its neighbours. I legend *scadman's heid*, I swallow the word *yoag*, I coin *butterfingersfish* that silk-lightning-slips from under the rock I lift and replace. Inquisitive little monkey, I reach under an overhang without due caution and, receiving a deep injection in the pad of my finger, yank back my wounded paw. Dog welks sumo-wrestle each other's tough albino feet. The water is lagoon-warm, skin a formality. I can *hear* the subtle myriads too, creaking, hissing and popping delicately, and when I spot an otter curled on a throne of *waar* like a bearskin hat, the air is still enough that I can hear it snoring. My awareness of past and future has fallen by the wayside. Like when people talk about a moment when desire got out of hand and say 'one thing led to another': the present moment grows and grows to encompass the sensing world, of intricate awareness, and was finally everything, a Now expanding in ripples, gathering the world to it by the armful

– until the shore all round begins to sizzle: snap, crackle and pop.

And now gradually the ocean begins to eject me with a subtle series of persuasions, as if forcing me back over crumbling bridges, Now leading to Now leading to Now, and I am not a 'we' any more, but a 'you' until all of a sudden you're hobbling across the grass on boot-shaped bones, and your hands are freezing, your legs soaked. The hill has swallowed the sun and is drawing itself to its full height. And it's like the comedown from a psychedelic drug: a peremptory eviction, a brusque shift in perception. Now the rich foraging grounds are nothing but mud and the trash of shells emptied by gulls. I see the land as visitors see it, as I suppose we all see it sometimes: a low snarl of exposed rock that hasn't yet escaped from winter, rock and treeless bog on a slatey sea. I'm too big for the rockpools now, too gallumphing for the tender pannacotta of the mudflats. The ebb shrugs me off to the drab winter colours of the hill: dead grass and frosty, lungy lichen.

If I met a neighbour now, could I find a word and work it to the tip of my tongue, strike it against the roof of my mouth, extrude it from my lips? Why, when I return to my rucksack, unscrew my thermos and take a slug of hot cocoa, and try to crook my numb fingers to write, do I find myself unable to begin, staring at the folded square of damp, spongy paper from my jacket pocket in something like disbelief, as if I was staring up from the floor of a deep pothole at a square of distant daylight?

I touch the nib to the paper, and lift it away again. I try a crass, bewildered word or two, as if learning a new orthography that my frozen fingers can hardly shape: tearing runes in the ruined paper that will prove to be illegible when I pore over them at home.

I am very cold. My fingers are swollen and ruddy from immersion in saltwater, from scrubbing barnacles and bristle-worms from the thick shells of mussels. Residual silt is trapped under them. Their scratched nails are chipped, like neglected chisels. I'm sunburnt and wind-burnt. The seat of my jeans is wet from crouching in the shallows as I sought the splurge-mouthed shell of a *smislin*. The doors in my brain are slamming shut behind me, pushing me to the forefront of my mind, like a pushy parent poking a child to the front of the stage. I shiver as I decant my welks, shoulder my personal portable portion of gravity, and put one foot in front of the other up the very real hill.

Bivalves are the most animated and expressive of sea-life. Before eating them, cockles need to be steeped overnight in a solution whose salinity is as close as possible to that of seawater. I crept through to the kitchen that night, waking the cat in his box for a quick soft word on the way, shining a torch into the Pyrex bowl where a periodic bubble bursting on the surface indicated that although all things were silent, as the folksong goes, not all mortals were at rest.

I heard a barely perceptible turbulence, the sound of a nosy parker's door opening a stealthy crack. First the translucent, glittering labia of the mantle, then, like the animated tongue of some Disney mutt, the bright orange foot swept left to right along the open shell. It looked like the cockle was licking its lips. Then, as if a bouncy castle was being inflated inside, the two siphons, each crowned with a delicate frill, pierced the billowing folds of the mantle. A deep submarine sigh, troubling the water. A cloud of silt and tiny pebble pumped out. It settled over the shells. Duped by the artificial salinity, the cockles were settling in, preening their soft tissues, questing for non-existent food: it is really best not to overthink it. I imagine them telling each other bedtime stories. *'It's funny ta tink at we've been on da sea-bed! An dat da watter'll creep in an hoid everything fae sight!'*★

★ 'Doon ida ebb', Peter Jamieson, *New Shetlander*, Summer 1973.

What We Talk About When We Talk About Solastalgia

MALACHY TALLACK

I.

We arrived in the autumn, as the warm days declined. We brought boxes filled with our respective pasts, and we stacked them in rooms that were not yet familiar. We merged our two lives in one place.

This was the first house we had shared, Roxani and I, and the first time either of us had lived in this town. We knew no one, and had little idea of our surroundings. Our only compass points were the supermarket, the train station, the hardware shop: practical places, each less than three minutes' walk away.

In those first few weeks, as we tried to turn this house into something we could call a home, our world shrank. The space within these walls was what we saw and what we talked about. The smell of emulsion, of white spirit, of wet plaster, was what we breathed. We stripped wallpaper, replaced skirting, laid carpets, built furniture. We took bare rooms and helped them hold the life we had imagined. We populated this place with ourselves.

Those days were mostly spent indoors, amongst the tools of our labour: the brushes and the scrapers and the innumerable Allen keys. And when these were put away, they were replaced in turn by cardboard, empty boxes strewn like the leaves that were falling, then, in the garden.

It was not always a happy time. The space between what was and what could be, the awful list of things undone, was always on our minds. Both hopeful and wearying at once, the focus on that work, that space, became a kind of narrowing. And so we made our way outside.

2.

Turn right from our front door, then right again, and you find yourself, feet scrunching, on a red gravel path that leads down to the river. It takes, at most, a minute from the house to the water, and some days each step feels like a sigh, a heavy breath expelled. The path goes on, beneath overhanging trees, then splits – one route hugs the riverbank, the other a long row of flowerbeds – before joining again beside a shallow weir pool. A little farther upstream, an arced footbridge, just wide enough for two, brings you to the opposite bank.

We have taken this walk almost every day in the months since we arrived. Most afternoons we turn back from that footbridge, along the other bank, a mile or so from door to door. But when the weather is good we continue: around the park that fringes the town, or else north along the river.

This repetition, this following in our own footsteps, began as a kind of escape, and it still serves that purpose. When we're tired, and our eyes ache from a morning in front of the computer, it always helps to walk, to go and then come back. But doing so like this – the same few routes, over and over – soon became something more. It became an intimacy.

3.

Things were drifting towards winter when we first began to walk, so we learned these paths in a time of disappearance, of contraction. Branches were sparsely covered, then bare, and birds were leaving, then gone. The perennials in the beds along the way died back, and the ground was dark and wet and cold. The river rose and grew faster.

This was, in some ways, the ideal time to get to know a place, when there is less to see and be distracted by. Everything felt stripped to its essence. We noticed the familiar, first of all. There were the birds that stayed throughout the year: the blue and great and long-tailed tits; the crows and magpies, rooks and jackdaws; the robins and the wrens. There were the dippers, with their broad, white bellies, that slipped like rain into the river. And every now and then there was a gallop and a gulp of blue. Kingfisher! The bird is gone before its name is even spoken.

Mid-winter, the white hellebores began to bloom, and the snowdrops not long after. The conifers – the pines and firs – were resolute throughout the short, light-lacking days. And even on the greyest afternoons, there was always a *readying* at work. No steady point of stillness or of balance, there was always expectation.

4.

We fell in love from a distance, Roxani and I, at opposite sides of an ocean. The times we'd spent together had always been punctuated by longer times apart. So to find ourselves here, in these months of presence, side-by-side almost every hour of the day, was a kind of luxury. It was also a kind of learning: the lessons of proximity.

Our walks became an extension of that learning. Day after day we reminded ourselves of what was here, of what we knew, and we tried to know more. We nudged each other towards noticing. *What will this bud become? What might those new leaves be?* We asked questions, looked for answers, and, where we could, identified. When spring arrived, we turned trees into wych elms and willows; we turned butterflies into small whites and orange tips. We tried to untangle the mesh of birdsong that hung between the branches.

This acknowledgement, this taking account of what belonged, was an act of care, and also of commitment. Over days, over weeks, over seasons, it was a process of coming-to-know. As the names we gathered for the things around us grew, our sense of where we were in turn expanded. An enrichment took place, an accumulation of knowledge and affection.

To be attentive, to be curious, to care: these are the makings of love. For love itself is a kind of expansion: a growth, and a willingness to grow. We knew this place better by knowing it together, by making it – in name and thought – a home. It is always a big word, that: *home*. And in those months, between us, it grew bigger.

5.

For more than a year before we came to this place, Roxani lived in a country in which armed conflict was an ongoing presence. Her work took her to places where few tourists would go, and where violence intruded on the everyday. She lived with those dangers, and I lived with the possibility of them from afar. I feared what could happen to her, and I imagined, repeatedly, the phone call that would bring me bad news.

Those months of worry, and of waiting, were not easy. They held familiar shadows. When I was sixteen years old, my father died, suddenly, and that memory still looms. Like many whose lives brought early encounters with grief, I know well the dread of losing what I care about, the anxious anticipation of absence. It lives in the chest, that feeling, lodged like a parasite between heart and lungs; and it guides the behaviour of its host. Too often, I have steered myself away from joy and from devotion. I have avoided what can be lost rather than risk the possibility of losing.

This was a fear that had always precluded love, a fear that had ensured loneliness, and that had led me, inevitably, towards regret. But in that time of separation, of counting down days from an ocean apart, I learned – having never previously understood – what it meant to muster hope, and to enact it, again and again. I learned, too, to see risk not as avoidable, but as imperative.

6.

Fear cannot be prised apart from love. Indeed, the possibility of loss, and the continued recognition of that possibility, is essential to the process of loving. It is part of what fuels that process. After all, the opposite of the dread I once felt in my chest is not love – not even close. It is complacency.

The lightness that wells at the sudden song of a wren is not a product of the melody alone, but of the silence that precedes it and that just as suddenly returns. The song is buoyed by its brevity. Likewise, the bright cumulus of a cherry tree is embellished by the knowledge that its blossoms soon will fall, and the honeyed warmth of autumn is sweetened by the imminence of winter.

Love, too, is lifted by lovelessness; it is made more present by the prospect of its absence. Love is sustained by the memory of what came before it, and the anticipation of an after. Fear, in this light, is not separable from gratitude. It is both incentive and reassurance. And this is where hope arises: in the knowledge that what is cherished can be lost, but that only through cherishing might that loss be averted.

7.

Now, together, our worries are mostly less immediate. They are the usual frettings of two people in their thirties, sharing a home. We worry about money, sometimes, and we worry about work. We worry about things that are bad in the world, and we worry that they will get worse.

Sometimes as we walk, we talk over what is troubling us: one speaks and the other listens, asks questions, and, when needed, reassures. We share what we've been working on, the words we've read and written; and in doing so we ease the knots that have tightened through the day. Our conversations are accompanied by the fuss and whisper of the river.

To get outside like this, to walk away from screens and deadlines, is to see our surroundings as both refuge and restorative. It is to find comfort in the movement of our bodies, and the presence of ourselves and each other in this place. It is the most ordinary of indulgences.

And yet, of course, this refuge is never truly divided from those things we might wish to escape. It is not possible or responsible to pretend otherwise. At least, not for long. And though we feel, always, the consolation of what's here – that sigh of wonder and relief – this place to which we turn is not empty of anxiety. To come to know it, as we have, is to see the ways in which it is vulnerable. To come to love it, as we have, is to encounter worry.

8.

Our first half-year in this house brought a deluge of dreadful news. Climate change, now seemingly unstoppable; waterways choked by plastic; the cataclysmic disappearance of insects; depletion, decline, extinction. While the gaze of these reports focused elsewhere, none of them excluded here. They described a damage from which no place is safe; they told of harms already upon us – harms that are only getting worse.

Amid the expanding lexicon of environmental catas-
trophe, it is no surprise that there are new words for
fear. After all, to pay attention to what is happening to
the world, and to imagine what might come next, is to
be afraid. It is to be struck, deep, by a double-hearted
horror. We, as human beings, are responsible for this
devastation; yet we, as individuals, are helpless to reverse
it. Both patient and pathogen, our suffering is guilt as
well as grief.

'Eco-anxiety', some call it – a term that has, at least,
the benefit of lucidity. 'Solastalgia', others say – which
does not. These words fix a label to the chronic alarm
that, increasingly, many feel. Like a lepidopterist's pin,
they fasten that feeling to the page. *Now*, they seem to
say, *we know what we are dealing with. Now we understand.*

9.

Worry is not an illogical response to the problems
that face the planet. Those problems are monu-
mental, and the more one learns, the harder it is to be
anything but horrified. To put a name to this worry is
an understandable urge. The magnitude of its cause, and
the sense of impotence it engenders, feel new. They feel
specific to the times in which we are living. And for
some, that specificity, that name, is a kind of comfort.
But for me, the opposite is true.

In the years I spent avoiding commitment to something or someone I could lose, I was never in doubt as to the problem. I knew dread was at the heart of it, and I knew, as well, where that dread had come from: the loss of my father, inescapable still. But to acknowledge that feeling and to call it mine did nothing to loosen its grip. To fixate on what was *particular* to my experience, while ignoring the ways in which loss, and the fear of loss, are in fact entirely *ordinary*, was to create a barrier to change. That change, in my case, came not from identifying specificity, but from recognising likeness.

The same is true, it seems to me, of the words we choose. These neologisms – eco-anxiety, solastalgia – are lines drawn in the air. They differentiate unnecessarily. And in doing so, in narrowing the lens like this, such words risk obscuring our best source of hope. What we talk about when we talk about solastalgia is fear. But what we talk about, as well, is love.

10.

In a week when Roxani was away, I walked the same few routes along the river. I went from home to home again, across the bridge and back, and on warmer days I went farther. I walked alone, but looked for the things we look for together. I noticed what was changing – the incremental shifts as spring turned into summer – and I noticed what stayed the same. My attention, it seemed to me, was never really mine alone.

This ongoing intimacy with place has bred an ongoing litany of concerns. Some are specific and immediate, while others are imprecise and look towards the future. There are times when I find myself pushing them aside, to keep from being overwhelmed. But it is never possible to do so for long. The fear is always present.

To say that there is hope to be found amid this fear, is not to say that disaster – climatic, ecological – can be averted. I am not at all convinced it can. Rather, it is to say that without *enacting* hope it is not possible to love. And without love, without cherishing what might one day be lost, then, truly, there can *be* no hope.

Mòinteach Leòdhais:
the Lewis Moorland

ANNE CAMPBELL

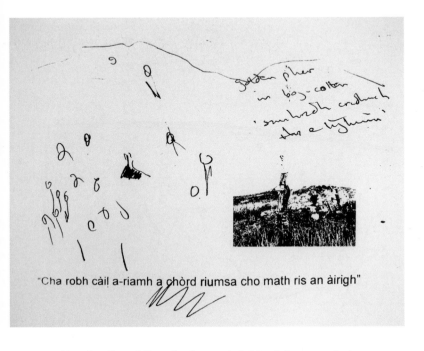

"Cha robh càil a-riamh a chòrd riumsa cho math ris an àirigh"

'Samhradh cridheach, the e a' tighinn' (screenprint)

'*Samhradh cridheach, the e a' tighinn*' (a hearty summer, it is coming) echoes the call of the golden plover in early summer. '*Cha robh càil a-riamh a chòrd riumsa cho math ris an àirigh*' translates as 'I never enjoyed anything as much as the shieling' and is a quote from my father, Kenneth Campbell, from the archive of Comann Eachdraidh an Taobh Siar.

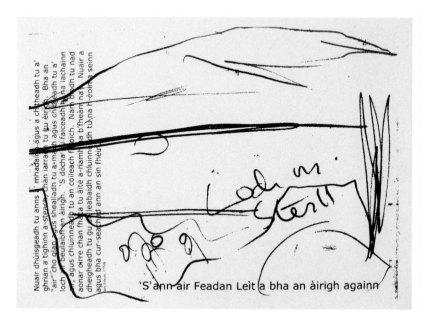

''S ann air Feadan Leìt a bha an àirigh againn' (screenprint)

'Our shieling was on Feadan Leìt.' 'When you woke in the morning and saw the sun coming in, you wouldn't wish to get up. The air was so clean and when you looked out you saw the loch in front of the shieling. You might see ducks, and you would hear grouse. When you were on your own there, you never saw a better place. When you went to bed you would hear the birds singing, and that was a pass-time in itself.' – John Campbell (Iain Ailean, Bràdhagair), Comann Eachdraidh an Taobh Siar archive.

The cold dark days of winter lay behind them and ahead were the lonely, lovely brown moors with their rushing streams and sparkling lochs. Shieling days were days of joy.

Donald Macdonald, *Dòrlach Ruan* (manuscript)

'Shieling days were days of joy' (screenprint)

The quote is from 'Lewis Shielings' by Donald Macdonald, *The Review of Scottish Culture* (*ROSC*) No 1, 1984. The inset photograph is my aunt Dolina, taken on the Lewis moor.

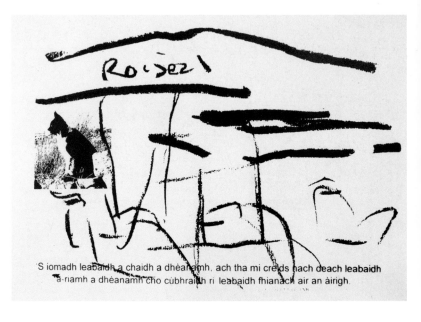

'A fragrant deer-grass bed' (screenprint)

'Many a bed has been made, but I don't believe any bed ever made was as fragrant as a deer-grass bed on the shieling.' – Kenneth Campbell (my father, Coinneach Isaac, Bràdhagair), Failt' air a' bhaile, BBC Radio nan Gaidheal, 5/12/84.

'Tha 'm bainne mar dh'fhàg thu 'n-dè e' (digital print)

'The milk is as you left it yesterday.' The text is from the song
'*A Phiùthrag 's a Phiuthar*'. In some versions of this song a sister is
trapped in a fairy hill: here she has been murdered at the shieling.
'Sister, oh sister, are you able to rise?
No, my love, I will never rise. The milk is as you left it yesterday,
the cattle and calves are amongst each other, the dairymaid missing,
the shepherd has not perished. My love was in charge of them.
Young man with the gun, give attention to my tale: I assure you
there is blood flowing from your shirt; it is not raven's blood, nor
deer's blood, but the blood of the dairymaid, you killed her
yesterday. A small sharp knife caused the injury, you let the blood
from her veins, it cut her sinews, and there was a little baby in the
crook of her arm.' (Words and translation from the sleeve notes
of Margaret Stewart's CD *Tògaidh mi mo Sheòlta*.)

'Nighean nan gamhna' (digital print)

'Girl of the year-old calves.' Text from the song 'Òran Tàlaidh an Each-Uisge' (lullaby of the water-horse). A water-horse (or a fairy lover) exhorts the (mortal) mother of his son to return to her child, which she has abandoned on the hillside without food or shelter.

(Words from 'The Shieling: Its Traditions and Songs' by Mrs Mackellar. Transactions of the Gaelic Society of Inverness 15. 1889.)

''S tu bhi marbh ann an innis na sprèidhe' (digital print)

'And you dead in the pasture of cattle.' Text from a song telling of
a young woman dead at the shieling, describing the blood flowing
through her shirt with no way of stopping it. (A. Macdonald,
'Songs of the Shieling', *The Celtic Magazine* 12:115. 1887.)

'Gheall mo leannan dhòmhsa cìr' (digital print)

'My lover promised me a comb.' Text from the song "*'Ille Bhig,
'ille Bhig Shunndaich Ò*', recorded from Christina Macpherson
of Scalpay, Harris by Donald Archie Macdonald, School of Scottish
Studies, Edinburgh, in 1963. 'This is a fairy song. It was said to have
been composed by a girl who was in love with a water-horse.
As the song describes, he was killed by her brothers. The song
lists some of the gifts he had promised to give the girl.'
(tobarandualchais.co.uk, track ID: 79470)

From *Ben Dorain:*
A Conversation with a Mountain

GARRY MACKENZIE

PART SIX:
RUT

*D*uncan Ban MacIntyre's In Praise of Ben Dorain *is an eighteenth-century Gaelic poem about a west Highland mountain and its herd of red deer. The work below combines an original translation of Macintyre's poem, on the left of the page, with new material on the right, to form a conversation between the 250-year-old poem and the modern world.*

Years later
I still think of them:
glorious

a gallus team
striding forth
in the flesh
of the moment

assembling
   to jostle and clatter
     up the cliffs –

between the moor with the naked birch
and the mouth of Fortress Corrie

they carry themselves like lords

   outside commerce
   outside property law
   the land is theirs
   and they serve it.

This is their paradise, enclosed by hills.
They wander up the sides of Bracken Corrie,
thread through the pass
to the field of hard water,
the plain we used to call
Wolf's Garden.

They browse at Willow Crag,
roam the northern slopes
where two ridges run
together like the cloven
halves of a hoof.

On the high moor

               where the autumn tides of grass
                   usher in the rut

the hinds are parading –

a matriarchal tribe
who tolerate the stags
for six weeks in a year.
The thrill of the season is on them

the stag is hefted
to a moving territory,
his harem in the hills;
they sport with each other,
  bound over moorland and moss

when a hind strays,
the stag brings her back;
when she slows
he lowers his head and tries
to lay his coarse chin on her rump.
Too early in oestrus.
She races off.
  They charge through bogs –

he rakes the ground
one antler at a time
and pisses in the wallow pool;
he fills his lungs
with its buttery
citric musk; he rolls
until his coat and the earth
and the whole glen (if he could)
are penetrated
with his presence.
  She becomes aroused

the stag, like a master of wine,

noses her vulva,
takes a sip of her
on his tongue,
draws back his upper lip
to better taste
her readiness.
They're a carnival of desire.
He licks her head, her neck,
the base of her tail.
She rubs her whole length
along his ribs,
working towards his rear
until she makes
to mount him.
Ben Dorain hosts a bacchanal:
now he mounts her
she stands

he mounts her
she stands

he mounts her
she stands

he mounts her
she stands

in the infinity
of herself,
the countless inter-

woven trails
of all that she is:
gladness, lust,
the scents of rut,
textures of fur
and grass in the gut,
pebble in a hoof,
iron in the blood,
the weight of the stag
as he mounts and thrusts.

At last she'll stand
in the queerness
of pregnancy,
one body
antlering into two.

The part of us that's deer
satisfies its thirst

on the slopes below Congregation Hill
where Annat Burn (the stream
of the chapel of an unknown saint)
brings its heather-honeyed water,
the hill's holy wine,
into the glen,

glistening
gushing
quickening

filtering as it flows
over its gravel bed,
sweeter than cinnamon
richer than cloves.

                Sometimes, Duncan Bàn, you'd think
                        that you couldn't sleep
               without the whispering songs
                 of the burns of Ben Dorain,
           the soft red noise of your soul;

           but for more than half your life

           you heard only carts on cobbled
               streets, the curfew beat
              upon guardsmen's drums,
                 the endless repeating
           anthems of economic growth.

Annat rises deep inside the earth,
  a never-failing tonic,
  abundant wealth
that can't be traded.

It flows between the arms
of the land's most majestic hills:
        listen
          the clear-
       flowing
      water

gentle–
  flavoured
   clear–
   headed
  water
bubbling and
 surging its
  way down
     hill from the
    shady
    springs

thamnobryum alopecurum   nestled in   foxtail feather-moss

  maidenhair pocket-moss   water–   fissidens adianthoides

   cratoneuron filicinum   cress   fern-leaved hook-moss

wry-leaved tamarisk-moss   liverworts   heterocladium heteropterum

   conocephalum salebrosum   moss   great scented snakewort

lean in and imagine you're carving a path
through this inch–high holy grove
where distinctions collapse in the shifting light, where
everything radiates everything else

The eddying pool
on the shoulder of Ben Dorain

is the pellucid music
of a chorus of bells:

 weightless
  melody

of water
ringing out
the silver

tongues

of the countless
burns
the larks

and the wings of
mining bees
landing

on yellow
flowers
madrigals

vespers
of the Ben
the piper's ground

embellished
and forever
coming into being:

Land of ditch and dell
hump and hillock
pillar and precipice

ruffled as the sea   rough-coated as a stag

matted with shoots and pastures of grass,
ganglia, cortex of steep, tufted paths

                      and the noses eyes ears
                of the hill, tooth, talon and wing,
              croziers, spikelets, radicles, roots,
            the great breaths of day and night

blossoming budbursting flowerblushing hill:
lightdappled greenmantled lifebuzzing hill:

from the heights of its slopes to the heart of its plains
this deer-land is decked
with riches with branches with creatures
with the world
thrumming through it —

Around Some Islands

AMANDA THOMSON

Within minutes of the boat leaving the harbour at Mallaig, I felt an untethering from ordinary life and place. *The Song of the Whale* sailed low and close to the water, the mainland receded only slowly, and any landmasses before us only gradually came into focus with an altered point of view. Eigg became unrecognisable as Eigg from the north, and Skye, from the south-west, became a fortress. Due west, Mingulay would emerge over the far horizon, first as a watery presence, only slowly becoming solid. This was an unhurried traversal, hours and hours of watching and looking. Fleckit skies. No phones, no internet. Shearwaters skimmed the waves in black to white to black lines, posses of guillemots bobbed on the swell and skittered away or ducked under as we passed. Wheens of puffins. Solitary tysties. I was on a 74-foot-long sailing boat, travelling around some islands with a group of people, most of whom would remain strangers, while two would become good friends. It's a trip that stays with me, in part because of the experience of slow journeying and hours only slowly unfolding. Days spent sitting, watching, thinking. We must have talked too, but I can't remember any of the specificities of conversation at all.

On these islands, the past, present and future are intimately intertwined, and each island offers up all times, if we know what to look for. There are abandoned crofts and townships where roofs and walls have fallen and sand and nature, or the machair, have encroached over doorways and into the crevasses between their stones. There are standing stones and prehistoric settlements; peat-banks that have been worked for generations, the remains of old field systems that we see when a low sun casts its shadows; rusting cars and ploughs and tractors: all testament to the longevity of human occupation and influence. On Canna there's a Celtic cross from around the eighth century, which is broken, so I was told, because it was used for target practice during the Napoleonic wars. Sailing around Canna towards Mingulay someone pointed back and spoke of a cave on the west side where the island's boys hid when the press gangs visited.

There's a bittersweet tension between humans and nature that is sometimes balanced, sometimes lost.

Canna's shearwater population was decimated because of the rats that came to the island, stowaways on boats over a century ago. Since the extermination of all 10,000 of them, the seabird colonies have seen a resurgence. Likewise the rabbit population, without predation, exploded and was perhaps upwards of 16,000 before thousands were culled in 2014. The rabbits not only affected agriculture on the island but their burrowing threatened to destroy the archaeological remnants of humans who, though long gone, have left traces hidden beneath the surface of the land.

These islands hold plants and birds that you would now be lucky to see and hear elsewhere in the UK. Red-necked phalaropes, corn buntings, storm petrels, eagles and divers of course, and it's on some of these islands that you might be lucky to hear the *crex crex* of the corncrake during the summer, calling from the midst of the tall grasses left for that purpose at the edges of fields. On some nights the gulls adjust their circadian rhythms to match the fishing boats that leave these islands before dawn.

Mingulay, more than all the other islands, was the one that felt most remote, unmediated, but also a place that had been left. Left behind and left to its own devices, despite the subtle marks that still remain, and that are so important to acknowledge, placing us in the grander, deeper, longer scheme of things. There is no ferry service to Mingulay or, for that matter, a harbour to allow an easy passage onto its land.

The Song of the Whale dropped anchor off the eastern side of the island, in the sheltered curve of the bay. From its deck we looked onto a sandy beach, a deserted village and the land rising beyond to a smoothly curved skyline. We could see the indents and humps of the lazy beds and the priest's house, a double-storeyed empty shell, sitting further up the hill and looking down on what had been the island's main settlement.

A dinghy took us to the shore. There, amongst the *lairachs,* the sand had piled in corners, and silverweed, thistles, ragwort and nettles inhabited the ruins. Since 1912 when the last inhabitant finally left the island, no one and nothing has stemmed the wear of the weather or the creep of the sand.

Though there were old fence-lines and the remains of dry-stane dykes, paths were scant, and no one told us where to go, or what to see.

Once on the island, three of us struck out from the bigger group, maybe sensing a welcome break from the confinement and togetherness of the boat. The possibilities of discovering for ourselves was important, I think, though while we started our walks separately, the natural geography of the island pushed us closer the higher we climbed, and we converged just before the top. A good friendship started right there on that walk, and I'm sure that it was this place and our shared experience of it, the wonder of the day, that cemented something before we even knew what it might become.

I should have guessed at the topology by the bonxies patrolling along the horizon line and how the sound of the swell of the sea rose, the sudden quickening of the air. But as we neared the shear of the hill up from the bay, I expected to see over to a dip that would take us down to the other side of the island, maybe to another beach. Instead I was met with nothing but air, cliffs and water – and seabirds wheeling and crying below me. My race, gender, class, age, the rest of the world seemed to fall away from me, just a little, and in that moment I was exposed, stripped back, just human. Here, below us, it was all birds: puffins and more puffins, guillemots and razorbills, fulmars wheeling high on the currents that push them up and over the cliffs so they sometimes startle, so fast and close and suddenly do they appear. This landscape, this seascape, these cliffscapes are vital, alive with movement and noise, and if you lean too far over the thrift-fringed edge of the cliff, perhaps to get a better view, or yet another photograph of a puffin, the reek of the guano rises to meet you. It is a place where you are both incredibly aware of yourself and where you are, at the same time, small and lost in its environment.

After the sedentary, rich passivity of the boat, here was the gift of hours to just walk, to sit on the west coast cliff-tops, or dip down steep promontories to see the puffins and razorbills which flew in and up, sometimes landing but often seeming to just tag the impossibly narrow ledges before falling away again. Perhaps they just didn't quite get the balance, the deceleration, the foothold they needed and had to fly off and around, come in again. We watched the paleness of the kittiwakes in bright sunlight against the dark cliffs in shadow, saw a shark basking in the waters below. Life pressed on life, and we entered into the lifeworlds of other species, overwhelmed by blue, black, white noise. It is estimated that there might be as many as 90,000 seabirds on Mingulay during the summer, and on the day I was there, there were perhaps thirty visitors on the whole island: our presence so fleeting. It was clear that everything would go on whether or not we were there, indeed, despite us being there and, as a gust whipped up to unsteady us and we found ourselves suddenly too close to the edge, or on a bank down to another cliff edge that was slippier, or steeper than we imagined, we knew how vulnerable, and how remote, how isolated we really were.

Later on, back in the bay, into and through the long gloaming we sat on the grassy banks above the beach, watching restless waves of puffins as they flew out across the water and circled and landed again and again until just beyond dusk.

In a forest, if you're paying attention, from a still start you can sometimes hear a breeze approach before it encircles and passes through and over you. In the same way, looking out over the Atlantic from a cliff-top, say, in Mingulay, or off Stoer Point in Sutherland, you can see squalls form at sea, and watch as they come in and soak you, or reach landfall a little way to the south or to the north. *Landlashed*. You're sometimes made aware, tangibly, of a near future soon to arrive. Might it be true that we see the future closer here on these islands than in other places?

AMANDA THOMSON

When I think about the landscapes of these islands, it is as much about the space around and above them, the vastness of the sky, the sea-salt wind coming off the Atlantic and the openness of the sea that can belie its power. Seton Gordon wrote, 'in its unhurried majestic speed, its tremendous strength, the Atlantic swell has its especial charm'. As we sailed from Skye to Canna to Mingulay the sun came out, there were gannets like harpoons into the water, the whirr of auks flying low over the water or bobbing with the waves and manx shearwaters speeding from trough to trough, gulls mobbing a distant fishing boat, and occasional terns too, and though we felt small and exposed, we were safe and secure and on top of things. And yet. In January 2005, the whole of the west coast was battered by a ferocious storm that did not abate for twelve hours. At its height the sea rose up two metres and a family of five in South Uist, fearing for their wellbeing where they were, tried to drive across a causeway to safety and were tragically swept away. I remember speaking with someone on Uist, six years on, who told me about this, who said that any time a storm was forecast, people feared that it would be like that nightmare storm of 2005, and what had happened then, and that fear was now something there and present in their lives. The island's inhabitants live with the human consequences of that storm and its aftermath, and perhaps they have already borne witness to what the future might contain.

In an article for Scottish Natural Heritage, Stewart Angus and James Hansom wrote, 'Climate change scenarios for NW Scotland and the Western Isles envisage a combination of rising sea level, increased winter precipitation and increased frequency and severity of winter storms.' Storminess. Ben Buxton tells us how in 1868 a huge wave washed over Geirum Mór (a small islet off the south-western tip of Mingulay that rises 170 feet above sea level) and swept away the sheep that were grazing there as it receded back to the sea. Extreme weather isn't new, but it may become more frequent, more ordinary, more regularly terrifying, and yet we live in a complicated world which seems full of ifs and maybes, possibles and probables, though that doesn't always dispel the realities of what we've seen can happen, has happened already. The poet Susan Stewart writes, 'We live, like the rest of nature, in the present; and we live as well, unlike the rest of nature, beyond the discernible horizon', and so we imagine, but we can't quite, quite, imagine.

There are places on the Uists and in other parts of the Hebrides and Western Isles where the water has come and pulled away at beaches to first expose lost and undocumented archaeologies, and then in its relentlessness swept those remains right out to sea. These islands hold a hope for greener energies, through wind, sun, waves, even seaweed. We consider the effects of the associated infrastructure on birdlife, on sub-aqua life, and weigh up pros and cons, sometimes environmentally, sometimes aesthetically, and come down on one side or the other. These islands give and take and we give and take: and we come, some stay, some go. Such places can sometimes feel too much and can sometimes hold too little.

Years have passed since that trip and though I have been close to other edges since, including Hermaness on Unst in Shetland, the most northern tip of Scotland, I've never quite had that same feeling again. I keep returning to the question of what it is to care (and I remember now that this is one of the ongoing conversations I have with the second friend I made on that boat trip). In places such as Mingulay, care was rooted in an awareness of how spectacular and special the place felt and should remain, and a personal vulnerability as I felt smaller and less in control, to take more care, especially knowing the ground fell away so near to where I stood. But I wonder what happens when we leave these places and return home to an altogether different place, where extremes are mediated and we are too busy to pay attention in the way I did, and could, on Mingulay.

The next morning we lifted anchor and sailed south around Berneray and the wind caught and pulled us north up the west coast of Mingulay towards Vatersay and Barra, and it was the steady cliffs that we'd looked over the previous day, bird-shit graffitied, that dominated the view. Cutting along the base of the cliffs, we saw unexpected nooks and caves and arches not readily seen from the top and I was struck by the contrast of the black cliffs in shadow and the flashes of the white of the gannets and kittiwakes as they drifted into sunlight and disappeared into shadow again. Though I knew that the colonies of auks and kittiwakes were teeming up there still, and I read somewhere that one cliff face can hold 5,000 birds, they were lost to us again.

Northern Raven

SALLY HUBAND

The clouds formed a white and solid layer of glare; all scale in the hill ground was lost. It felt both oppressive and freeing. I followed the burn upstream but stopped before the ravine and looked for the nest with my binoculars. The nest sits on a rocky ledge that over-hangs the dark and peaty water of the burn that flows down the hill for only a short distance before meeting the Atlantic Ocean. It is a vast and sprawling structure: gnarled stems of old-growth heather are woven through with brightly coloured plastic fishing net twine, marine litter gathered from the shore, but the wool-lined depres-sion in which the raven sits is small and cups her body so tightly that her tail feathers are pushed almost upright.

I could not see the male anywhere but he had been watching me. A single rasping call cut through the distance between us. It felt like a warning. I turned and began to follow the burn downstream to the ocean, my pace quickening as his calls grew louder. When he landed nearby on a prominent boulder, I halted too. For a moment we faced each other in silence, and then he dipped his head low, stretched out his neck and called and called. The female lifted from the nest and, as if tethered to her, the male took flight and followed her to a distant green slope of re-seeded ground. I continued downstream, pausing only to take the fresh pellet that the male raven had left behind on the boulder.

At home, I spread newspaper on the kitchen table and began to dissect the raven pellet. It was mostly composed of deep green moss flecked through with tiny shards of pale and brittle lichen, all bound together by strands of fine white wool. Between the squeeze of my thumb and forefinger I could feel the resistance of bone. Field mouse bones, perhaps. A dull shine led me to the jointed leg of a spider and soon I had a full set. I used tweezers to gently extract the spider's carapace from the tight hold of the pellet.

In that instant, I imagined myself to be the spider and the tweezers became the sharp hook of a raven's beak bearing down. I set the tweezers down on the table and wondered why, in my mind, I had become the prey and not the predator.

Here in Shetland, ravens seem to shadow us through the ages. We can almost measure ourselves in some way against these birds. In 1615, the Shetland court issued a statute which required landowners to present the heads of ravens and other pest species. In 1616, the same court issued the sentence of execution for the crime of witch-craft to Jonet Dynneis, Barbara Scord and Katherine Jonesdochter. These women were strangled and then their bodies were burnt on a prominent hillside for all to see.

Now, four hundred years later, licences are granted to allow the killing of ravens to protect livestock. Only a few licences are issued in Shetland each year but it is probable that more ravens are killed than licences allow. Now, also four hundred years later, much remains to be done to end violence against women in Shetland. In common with small rural communities elsewhere, many survivors of rape in Shetland do not contact the police. In the 2017–18 reporting period, Shetland Rape Crisis supported forty-four clients. Shetland Women's Aid supported 284 women and children between 1 April and 30 November 2018. By late October, in the same year, a further sixty-seven women and children were on this organisation's waiting list.

Violence against women is a cause and consequence of inequality. In Shetland, the raven has become a symbol, of sorts, of this inequality. On the last Tuesday of each January, the Shetland Islands Council flies a raven banner – a red flag with a black heraldic raven – from the height of the town hall to mark the occasion of a community festival, the Lerwick Up Helly Aa. This is the largest and most spectacular of Shetland's twelve Viking-themed fire festivals, each of which breaks the dark months of winter in a blaze of fire and revelry. In Lerwick, over 900 men march through the streets of the town bearing fire in a procession that ends with the burning of a Viking war galley, a replica longship, in the municipal playpark next to the town hall.

The Lerwick town hall is also rich in raven imagery. The first foundation stone of this building was laid on 24 January 1882 and that evening the very first Lerwick Up Helly Aa torchlight procession took place. The coat of arms of Lerwick Burgh was also granted in 1882 and features a sable raven and a Viking war galley, to signal the 'distinctively Northern'[*] identity of these islands. This raven of 1882 was transplanted onto the Shetland Islands Council's coat of arms in 1975.

The emblematic ravens of the Lerwick Up Helly Aa and of the Shetland Islands Council all vary in their appearance: spread-eagled and heraldic, bloody in beak and claw or sleek and digital. But in 2019, they have all come to represent the same thing, a distinctively northern form of sexism.

Women and girls have asked to join the Lerwick festival's torchlight procession but they are not allowed. Or so says the Lerwick Up Helly Aa committee, a committee made only of men. Back in 1902, some women did secretly join the town's procession, their identities hidden by their guizing costumes. The committee at this time 'put its foot down on this experiment'[†] with such force,

---

[*] *Arthur Laurenson, his Letters and Literary Remains – a Selection*, edited by Catherine Spence, published in 1901 by T. Fisher Unwin, London, p. 70.

[†] *Up Helly Aa: Tar Barrels and Guizing – Looking Back*, by C.E. Mitchell, published in 1948 by T. & J. Manson, *Shetland News* Office, Lerwick, Shetland, p. 152.

it would seem, that for some people, excluding women and girls has become almost as much of the event's purpose as the torchlight procession itself.

Elsewhere in Shetland, participants in the rural Up Helly Aas have been pointedly proud to highlight that women and girls march alongside men and boys. Only the Lerwick event has become embarrassingly singular in defending, in the name of tradition, the importance of an all-male procession. In the Lerwick community event, women are only allowed to spectate, sew costumes or serve food in halls.

Few people dare to speak up, to call for girls and women to be included in the Lerwick event; it's not worth the hassle. I didn't at first but then something inside of me snapped. I read the words of a woman who described how it felt to be excluded as a young girl from the junior event when she was at school in Lerwick. Then my three-year-old daughter came home from pre-school singing the words of the Up Helly Aa song and wearing a cardboard helmet, shield and torch. Her older brother, not judging but just reflecting on what he had seen in Lerwick, told her that girls could not be Vikings. She looked gutted, and confused.

For the most part, the Lerwick Up Helly Aa is much enjoyed by locals and tourists alike. It is an incredible spectacle. Over nine hundred fire-carrying guizers march through the streets of the town. But the more that I have learnt about the Lerwick festival the more my anger has grown. I know of women who have stopped going to the halls for the evening's entertainments because they are tired of being sexually harassed. After I spoke out, with others, to call for the festival to move with the times, a woman told me that her vagina was grabbed without her consent during the festival. I heard more stories like this and so did others. One account of a more serious sexual assault made me feel sick to my stomach. It is clear that some men equate the Lerwick Up Helly Aa with a night of sexual entitlement.

The Lerwick festival could not take place without the support of the Shetland Islands Council. The council, supported by Police Scotland, close roads and provide venues including both primary schools and the municipal playpark in which the ship is burnt. The council extends licensing hours and declares a Shetland-wide public holiday the day after the event. On the day itself, inside the town hall the Convener of the Shetland Islands Council hosts a civic reception for the Guizer Jarl, the chief Viking, and his squad.

The Jarl, a different man each year, wears a helmet decorated with the tattered black wings of a raven and the design on the shield he carries matches the bloody-beaked raven in the town hall's Up Helly Aa stained-glass window. During the day of the festival, the Jarl with his squad of men, and the Junior Jarl with his squad of boys, visit the town's primary schools. Pre-school and primary-aged girls and boys watch as their headteachers warmly welcome a community event in which sexism is overt and defiant into their settings.

In 2018, a group of secondary school students from Lerwick, four girls, applied to form a squad in the 2019

Junior Lerwick Up Helly Aa. Their application was refused because they were girls. The Junior Jarl Squad was still invited into the atrium of their school on the day of the Lerwick Up Helly Aa and for some students, staff and parents alike, this felt like a sore blow.

Because the Lerwick Up Helly Aa committee stonewalls any requests to allow women and girls to march, in 2019 a group of us asked the council to help, to act as an intermediary. It is their legal duty after all. The Public Sector Equality Duty element of the 2010 Equality Act requires public bodies to work towards eliminating discrimination and to advance equality of opportunity. When asked to begin this process, to work collaboratively to end the discrimination, the council instead initiated a complaints process. Before the process was completed, the Chief Executive rushed to release a statement to the *Shetland Times*. The statement was defiant. The council's involvement in the festival was viewed, by the council, as legal. When the council's investigation response was later released, there was not a single reference to the Public Sector Equality Duty.

Sexism is institutionalised. It always was, but in this moment it became formalised. The raven banner shifted into an overt declaration of sorts, one that was hostile towards the girls and women who had dared to ask to take their places in their community festival. The council's response: another form of silencing.

In the months following, bruised and a little in shock, I began to spend more time watching ravens, as if to reclaim them away from all this. I didn't have to go far.

In late March, I drove slowly past a garden tree near my children's school. Through the shadowy thicket of branches, I could see the thick bill of a female raven poking above the rim of her nest and I felt a surge of hope.

Each April in Shetland, licensed bird ringers check raven nests for occupancy. This year I joined one of the ringers. We drove a circuit of the Mainland and the ringer described the history of each nest that we visited. This nest, he explained, is repeatedly pulled down. This nest, where a frozen fall of twigs and lamb bones tumbled down through the branches of a tree, was felled by the wind. This nest, in the stream gully, is where the crofters take a positive interest in the ravens' productivity. At this nest, in a quarry, someone waits until the young are almost big enough to fledge and then throws them all out of the nest still alive.

One nest was low enough for us to scramble up to. Both ravens peered down at us from a cliff-top above, calling without pause at the intrusion. There were six eggs in the nest, eggs surprisingly small for a bird which has a wingspan of over a metre. They were lightly speckled and the colour of the deep blue-green of a shallow sea that overlies shell sand.

At the next nest, the ravens did not retreat so far. The female left her eggs and joined her mate a metre or so above the nest. He wielded a stone in his beak as if in warning. As the nest was checked, the raven dropped the stone and took flight to lunge at the ringer with his talons. The female stayed put and frantically ripped up grass until her beak was brown with mud.

Then, in early May, I joined a team of two ringers at a raven's nest near my house. The six eggs that this nest had held were gone, replaced by three beaked bags of skin. The nestlings were beautiful and a bit grotesque. Dark fluffy down covered their bodies but underneath bald grey skin stretched tightly over huge distended bellies. Neat rows of white sheathed pin feathers trimmed their stubby wings. I expected to be pecked and bombarded with low rasping screeches, or shit, but the nestlings were calm and quiet. They lay still on the grass with their beaks clamped shut and unblinking grey-blue eyes. The deep downturn of their yellow gape made them look funny, grumpy even, but their talons were already intimidating, black and scaled and sharply clawed. The adult birds wheeled above us, jet black in a deep blue sky, primary feathers splayed wide. They called without break and at times they seemed to momentarily suspend flight, one bird lying over and almost enclosing the other, as if to offer comfort.

We visited the tree nest too, in the garden near my children's school. There was only one young raven and it was perched on the edge of the nest as if on the brink of fledging. I held it gently to the ground whilst the ringer fetched a ring and a set of pliers from the back of the van. It stayed quiet and didn't move at all when an adult bird appeared overhead and called as if distressed.

At the end of May, I checked on the nest in the garden

tree again. The single fledgling sat quiet and watchful on a branch next to the nest. She or he was still a little short in beak and tail but sat so supreme, black feathers gleaming in the sun. I felt enamoured of this bird that I once briefly held in my hands. The adults were nowhere to be seen. I checked again a week later, in early June, and the fledgling had left too.

I will never free ravens from all that they have come to mean in Shetland – the council's enabling of patriarchal control and male sexual entitlement, and the institutionalisation of sexism in Lerwick schools, all a permission of sorts for misogyny – there is still too much work to be done. But one day, on the last Tuesday of January, girls and women will also carry fire through the streets of Lerwick, alongside boys and men. Either that or the Lerwick Up Helly Aa in its current form will die and something better will be born from its ashes.

The Ruling Class

JESS SMITH

Scotland's windswept heather glens and snow-capped mountains, where balladeers sang of lonely lovers and broken clansmen limped home to low-roofed crofts after a long journey, is also the kingdom of the mighty red deer.

The red deer exist amid these magnificent heights, indigenous like the proud Celtic warriors who once ran barefoot across stone and peat to swim in the ice-cold waters of scattered lochans.

In the lower region of the forest floor, ambushed by bog and green marshes, it is easy to imagine the haunt of the mythical cross-legged Broonie of childish nightmares. Caledonian pine cradling osprey nests of stick and twig grow side by side with the ancient oaks believed to have been planted when the Romans left Scotia's shores.

Rowan trees sprout from stone crags, defying the natural process of ground-held roots. Yet they grow healthily to scatter red berries across a sea of moorland and open countryside to feed flocks of visiting fieldfare.

Where jagged cairn locks horns with thunderclouds and eagles soar, there is no other place on earth more fitting a terrain for the herds of Highland Scotland.

One may wander among their territory for weeks and see neither hide nor hair of them. However this all changes at the rut, when the hinds are in season and a king is chosen. He must challenge and be challenged. Numbers can range from a few dozen to thousands but only one can dominate. At such a crucial time it would be a mistake to judge these usually quiet and shy animals as mild and meek – make no mistake, there is an intelligent savagery about the battle for control. It is precise, with no room for error. Mother Nature in her wisdom manages this powerful conflict: she has given the warriors their weapons, which grow like iron spikes from their rigid skulls.

High upon the tops an early warning of winter had sprinkled a dusting of November snow. The rut had begun!

Across mountainous glens, braesides and thick forests and by deep lochan banks, the mating call can be heard for miles. The monarchs were on full alert. Their royal position was under threat. Challengers for the throne lined up to take control.

Twixt two formidable mountains the herd thudded flat the heather and dying bracken. Loose stones broke away from crags of jagged rock, rolling like thunder from almost vertical braes.

Who knows where the young stag appeared from, but he desired this harem, craved the territory and he was there to fight for it, a right afforded by Nature herself.

He had prepared well in advance by urinating across the bracken, leaving his smell on tree trunks and any place he could spread a trail for the harem to follow. Eager to womb another generation of their species, the hinds followed, as many as he'd ever seen, ready and willing to give their adoration to the future monarch of the glen. Each nosed his aroma, thick on the breeze.

His body stiffened as the rhythm of his loins grew ever more intense. The oncoming fury with the master would determine his strength and a wisdom offered to Nature's chosen few. Others have failed: heavier, more powerful stags. What made him think that he might succeed?

His youthful lungs swallowed the sweet air; each breath sent testosterone racing through his body like mercury boiling to its limit.

The 'play' was imminent. He was never more ready to act it out.

Antlers thrashed the ground to lift and tear heather from its peaty roots, mixed with clumps of sphagnum moss. He roared from the pit of his stomach. From a distance he knew that he looked and sounded the part of a muscle-bound warrior, a mighty foe. Perhaps though, to the main player's eye, one who had not yet mastered the art of deception. Was he just giving an appearance of a larger than normal beast or was he, in truth, a serious challenger? Would the mighty monarch see him as a worthy opponent or perhaps nothing more than a fly in a spider's web, easily caught and disposed of?

The youngster had made his decision. To run away would be futile: it was rut time; the master of the herd would chase and trample him to death. He had to carry his battle plan forward. He roared from the pit of his stomach, so loud that it echoed along the river and across the glen.

The sound pierced the ears of the God-like ruler who stood erect on a jagged pinnacle of grey and white quartz stone. Who was this young buck that would take on the father of the herd without awareness of his formidable might? It was unlike a stranger to approach; yet not one of his seed surely?

From his viewpoint the old stag could see how his youthful opponent held himself. Unlike his own sixteen-pointers, the young stag had only twelve-pointed antlers but that didn't mean weakness: it was how he used them that mattered.

Silently the master of the Highlands approached, carrying his heavy antler-bound head like a jewelled crown. He'd sharpened his crowning glory into needle-points for this battle to remain chieftain of his clan. There was too much at stake. One one wrong move and his reign would be over.

From the corner of his eye the young stag watched

the mighty beast step down from his vantage point of quartz, circle a patch of stony ground and snort the air.

Thumping heartbeats, loud as thunder inside his head, awakened every hair of his hide to stand stiff along his spine.

For one tiny moment fear crawled inside his testosterone-filled arteries to momentarily cool his ardour. Here stood a mountain of a stag. Rays of intermittent sunshine glistened through those sharpened antlers like a headful of Highland dirks. But it was too late. The duel was imminent.

Avoid those pointers, he warned himself, but only the learned know how. He had little experience, had never fought before. A young 'nose to the wind buck' without knowledge would come out bleeding, that's for sure!

He had wandered among several herds before settling on this crown. Watched others take on those red giants, picking up on their movements, sidestepping the torso stabs, and learned that heavy breathing and snorting nostrils told a tale of weakness – if there was the slightest sound of broken rhythm in both the snort and the breath, he might falter and fall!

That day neither master nor student failed to show any resistance to the oncoming crash of antlers. They faced each other full on. Heads were raised high on strong stiff necks as each roared from way down in his throat. Their thick manes of blackish brown bristled and shimmered in the dawn sunrise. The main bout was imminent!

For weeks lesser deer had tackled each other. Young stags had fought while the chief watched from his vantage point upon the pinnacle of rock. Instinctively he knew who would cause him problems but there had been none to worry him until this strong-backed stranger arrived. This youngster who had moved along his borders had been eyeing him up for days. He'd watched him sniffing the harem. There would be a fight but would the young stag have enough courage to see it through to the end? His strong muscled legs, stiff back and penetrating black eyes seemed already to be walking in the monarch's footsteps and he held his head high, a sure sign of the pride which both had in abundance.

For a minute they stood at a safe distance and stared eye to flashing eye; then the battle began. For over an hour they fought, enraged with raw male dominance, locked together with nothing but brute strength.

No man or beast could have intervened in such a fight. Every thud of head, turn of body was driven by raw power of muscle and bone as they rammed against any tree trunk that got in their way. Even the jagged rock did not hinder that almighty struggle for the crown.

It should have been the challenger's crown; he was younger, stronger, powerful. The chieftain's plaid was ripped and torn; he should have fallen but for one single factor!

Wisdom gave the old master an advantage. Not the sharp points to his antlers, but the fact that he knew the terrain, the secure rocks and where to sidestep. What a force he used against the youngster to ram his left side, lifting him into the air so high that he lost all balance!

Over and over he tumbled off the precarious cliff edge, like a thistle-head being blown on the wind, like drift-wood toppling from a raging waterfall.

His fight was over; the king would rule for another year.

Remarkably the young buck found his footing, he leapt on several narrow ledges and survived. But he was cut, broken and in pain. He limped onto the secluded forest floor. The battle was well fought; he'd lost to a wiser foe. He wandered far, took security behind a granite roofless ruin amid dead bracken and sapling pine to lick his open wounds.

He would join that clan but only when his opponent allowed it. And if a poacher's gun or gamekeeper's fancy didn't cut short his life-force, he'd face his lord and master once again in the coming year, as a wiser, stronger buck. He had not challenged the monarch without learning wisdom from he of the mighty antlers, his *cabar feidh*.

Stags too injured and old will become loners and roam at will. Perhaps some will remain with the herd but only at a distance. Those aged and too far gone will give up the ghost in some secluded bog where Mother Nature directs her buzzards, red kite and raven to feast upon their flesh. And when the bog spews up their bones, the sun will bleach them bonny.

Young stags and those veterans of a similar battle will stay within the confines of a 'male-only club' and toe the line.

Winter's frosted drum will bang for the chieftain to guide his pregnant harem to lower ground away from the bitter chill of north winds.

Life within the clan will centre around feeding and survival until spring sends them upwards to live in relative peace on the higher slopes.

Unlike man, their only predator, red deer do not harbour grudges. They do not pick quarrels or remain within the herd with aggressive tendencies.

They simply know and live by the rules.

When the rut returns, Mother Nature's easel will be in place with purple and crimson flashes of paint to splash her canvas.

No mortal will eye her portrait: that honour she has given over to the red deer of Scotland's mountains and glens.

It is their story.

At Diarmaid's Grave

DOUGIE STRANG

The track to Cunside below Ben Loyal was wet from the morning's rain. Two roe deer crossed it ahead of me and slipped into the birch wood; they were so fluent in their movement it was hard to be sure of them. It was late afternoon, the sky had cleared, and the October sun was low on the moor. I was halfway through a month of walking in Assynt and Sutherland, and Ben Loyal was the northern pivot around which my walk would turn. The month away was timely: I'd turned fifty; my children were teenagers, beginning to shape their own lives; my work was flexible; and my wife and I both understand the gift of space.

The names have slipped. Ben Loyal is really Beinn Laghail, the Gaelic in turn derived from *laga fiall*, Norse for 'law mountain'. Cunside is from Ben Loyal's northern spur, Sgòr Chaonasaid. The meaning of the word is unclear, but the great spike of it looms with certainty above what remains of Cunside farm.

In the summer of 1957, the poet and folklorist Hamish

Henderson followed the same track out from the Kyle of Tongue. He was travelling through Sutherland with the Stewarts of Remarstaig, an extended family of Gaelic-speaking Travellers, who tin-smithed and hawked their wares in the crofting townships of the north-west Highlands. Hamish was recording traditional songs and stories for Edinburgh University's School of Scottish Studies, and he described that summer on the road with the Stewarts – with their horses, carts and bow tents – as the high point of his life. While they were camped at Brae Tongue, he walked over to Cunside, looking for Uaigh Dhiarmaid, 'Diarmaid's Grave', which he'd been told lay at the foot of Ben Loyal. Hamish failed to find the grave that day, and later expressed regret that he never had the chance to return and try again.

Nowadays, Cunside is a semi-derelict cottage and byre, with a grass infield protected by a dry-stone dyke that has tumbled in places. The nearest neighbour is the farm at Ribigill, two miles away. The birch wood, where the roe deer disappeared, surrounds the infield to the north and east, its trees twisted with age; moorland stretches west to Ben Hope, merging with A' Mhòine, the great moor that lies between the Kyle of Tongue and Loch Eribol.

When I arrived at the cottage its front door was open. I propped my rucksack by the doorway and stepped inside. Swallows' nests were cupped to ceiling joists; sheep shit was thick on the stone flags in the kitchen. In the front room, a sofa had fallen backwards through rotten floorboards, its cushions split, spilling horsehair and a tangle of rusted springs. A table lay collapsed in the corner, the turned wooden legs riddled with woodworm. There was no wiring, no switches or sockets, and nothing was made of plastic – a house from before the Anthropocene. Three layers of wallpaper peeled off a wall in the front room, each layer revealing ever more delicate flower and foliage patterns.

The stairs to the attic were worn thin in the middle of each step, the footfall of those who'd lived there pressed into the wood. There were two wood-panelled bedrooms in the attic, both empty. I climbed back downstairs, stepped out into the evening and went looking for Diarmaid's Grave. I had an advantage over Hamish: before I began my walk I'd researched and found that the earliest edition of the Ordnance Survey map for that part of Sutherland marked exactly where the grave lay, just beyond the shelter of the dyke, at the edge of the moor. I dug out from my rucksack my modern OS map and checked where I'd pencilled an X. I followed the dyke west and then north, searching down the line of it. The grave was obvious when you knew where to look, berthed in the land like the upturned keel of a boat, turf covered, twenty-five feet long and three feet high in the middle, its prow pointing towards Ben Loyal. Yellow hawkbit was in flower amongst the turf.

It's a familiar story: an old, powerful man marries a young, beautiful woman. In this case, the old man is Fionn mac

Cumhaill, brooding, irascible, a hero in decline. Gráinne, his new wife, elopes with her guileless lover, Diarmaid, and Fionn seeks revenge, compelling Diarmaid to hunt a monstrous boar. Diarmaid kills the boar but Fionn, in his treachery, insists that Diarmaid measures the corpse by pacing its length, and the sole of one of his feet is pierced by the boar's poisonous bristles. The story is over a thousand years old, though its roots go back further still, and there are numerous Diarmaid's Graves in Scotland and in Ireland, testament to the popularity of the tale and to the way that these old stories migrate. The Gaelic-speaking people who settled at Cunside anchored their belonging with the tale of Diarmaid, embedding it in the landscape so that who they were became part of where they were.

I was standing on the mound. A cluster of red deer hinds, thigh-deep in autumn bracken, watched me from the moor. The bracken glowed orange in the sunset. Ben Loyal was in shadow above me, Sgòr Chaonasaid and the other peaks jutting like fangs from the dark jaw of its ridge. I'd no idea what lay beneath me. Stories attach themselves to ancient sites, building layers of meaning that aren't always consistent with the archaeology. The mound at Cunside is ambiguous: it might be the remains of a Bronze Age cairn, or the grave of a Viking raider who sailed up the Kyle, or simply a pile of stones, cleared from the infield by early settlers. It doesn't really matter. What matters is that those who'd lived at Cunside *knew* that this was Diarmaid's grave, and that his story put them in their place.

In the 1970s, under the direction of Alan Temperley, their English teacher, the pupils of Farr Secondary School along the coast at Bettyhill set out to gather local tales as remembered by the last Gaelic-speaking crofters and villagers between the Kyle of Tongue and Strath Halladale. The version of Diarmaid's tale they recorded has lost much of its complexity. No names are given, or reference to the elopement; all that's remembered is the terror of the boar, the warrior who came north to hunt it, and their confrontation on Ben Loyal. When the warrior kills the boar and casts it from the summit of Sgòr Chaonasaid, its tusks gouge the side of the mountain as it falls. This scarring on the north face is still known as Sgriob an Tuirc, 'the Furrow of the Boar'; a stream gathers in it and bears its name, flowing down past Cunside.

The hawkbit flowers on the mound were clear and bright, cupping the last of the sun. I needed to make camp and considered sleeping in one of the cottage's attic rooms, where I could brush the floor clear of broken glass from the skylight, and lay out my mat and sleeping-bag; but the eeriness of the abandoned house would be magnified by the dark. So I went to the birch wood instead, and found dry, level ground to pitch my tent. I gathered dead branches, lit a small fire and cooked stew in a pot. The night thickened around the fire. I drank whisky from a tin cup.

Having given up his search for Diarmaid's Grave, Hamish Henderson sought the shade of the birch wood and took a nap in the heat of the summer's afternoon. I pictured the big man curled in the grass close to where

I was camped. He would have been thirty-eight. I knew him in his late seventies, when I was a student at the School of Scottish Studies and he was Honorary Fellow, so my image of the younger man asleep was overlaid by memories of him loosened by age, hair thin and white under his famous tweed hat. Hamish writes that when he opened his eyes, a roe deer fawn was watching him from a few feet away, until he stirred and broke the moment, and it ran off.

When my fire was down to embers, I sipped the last of the whisky and toasted Hamish; then I crawled into my tent. It was rut month and red deer stags bellowed their claim to the moor throughout the night. Geese flew overhead, arriving for the winter, the noise of them a comfort: their funny, convivial honking; the beat of their wings steady, like breathing. The clear sky dropped the temperature and I felt grateful, and guilty, for the goosedown in my sleeping-bag. In the morning the floor of the birch wood was silver and gold with frost and dead leaves. I boiled water on the stove, packed away my tent, then sat drinking tea, looking out from beneath the trees at the infield and the moor beyond. A raven perched itself on one of the copestones that topped the dyke, its wings glossy in the brightness of the morning. It hopped along a few stones, casually, then dropped out of sight on the other side.

This is a contested landscape. Some would see the moor rewilded, with deer numbers reduced and trees planted, their roots reaching down to the bones of wood-land that was here before; others would put wind farms on the ridges, build power-lines to send the electricity south; others still would reverse the Clearances, bring people back to the land, place ownership in the hands of the communities who live here. If Lockheed Martin gets its way – and planning permission is currently being sought – A' Mhòine will become the site of the UK's first spaceport, with a launch pad built in the middle of the moor, from which satellites will be rocketed into space. I wondered what those who'd lived at Cunside might make of such a thing, or what Hamish might. He'd probably take the long view, maybe compose a song about it, a satirical song likening the spaceport to other expensive follies that have come and gone, causing barely a ripple in what he called 'the carrying stream', that fine metaphor for the deep culture of people and place: a stream whose surface shifts and reshapes through time, but whose current endures.

I leaned my rucksack next to Diarmaid's Grave, and walked to the stream that marks the boundary between the farm and the moor, the narrow stream that flows from Sgriob an Tuirc. Hamish's metaphor sparkled in the sun before me. I fished out an image of Diarmaid, pale and cold, the boar's poison in his veins. In the story, Fionn, full of remorse for what he's done, scoops water in his healing hands, but when he returns to tend to Diarmaid, jealousy is a great spike in his heart, his hands loosen and the water slips away. He tries again, and a third time, finally returning with the water unspilt; too late, Diarmaid, bright flower of the Gael, is dead. According to the tale, he's buried side by side with the boar, a nod to those older roots of the story, where we find that the pair are half-brothers, the one given the form of a wild animal. So it was for those who lived at Cunside: mindful that we humans aren't the only protagonists in the landscape, their stories acknowledge the need to respect and accommodate what lies, untamed, beyond the dry-stone dyke.

I filled my water bottle from the stream and gathered an armful of stones from the rubble of a tumbled section of the dyke. I made a small circle on top of the grave mound amongst the turf and the hawkbit flowers, placing a rough, heart-shaped stone in the middle, for Diarmaid, for Hamish; then I hoisted my rucksack and followed the stream up onto the slopes of Ben Loyal.

I focused on the graft of gaining height, veering left to track the course of another stream, Allt Chaonasaide, up to the bealach between Ben Loyal and its neighbour, Ben Hiel. Birch and rowan clung to the banks of the stream. I heard the sharp *tisk tisk* of a wren above me, reluctant to cede the way, flitting ahead a few yards then turning back to stare me down, defending its patch as spiritedly as any stag. A bright gang of fieldfares, winter migrants, charged from tree to tree. The stream became a series of pools and falls as the hill steepened.

From the bealach, the profile of Ben Loyal is less fanged and more like crumbling molars in need of care, with Loch na Creige Riabhaich, 'the Loch of the Brindled

Crag', a cavity beneath the ridge. I left my rucksack on an outcrop below An Caisteal, Ben Loyal's highest peak, and walked north along the ridge to Sgòr Chaonasaid. Spent deer grass and moss gave way to stone – granite tors, jutting at angles; great slabs of rock, pocked with lichen. I was light-headed with the release of the weight of my rucksack, and with the views that swirled around me as I clambered up the topmost tor. The Kyle of Tongue was a blue-grey ribbon, twisting inland, cut by the dark line of the causeway; cars crossing it were like scurrying beetles, their shells glinting in the sun.

In a hundred years, when the seas have risen and the Kyle has swamped the causeway, I doubt we'll still be sending rockets into space, chasing dreams that, having scuttled the earth, we might jump ship and head for the stars. I suspect instead that the ruins of the spaceport, the rusting spike of its rocket launcher, long since scavenged of anything useful, will be an eyesore to the people who are once again working the land at Cunside, carting seaweed from the Kyle to fertilise the infield, hunting the deer that slip so fluently into the birch wood, telling their tales of Diarmaid and the monstrous boar that he fought on the mountain above them.

A blanket of cloud was being pulled north and east from Assynt, covering Ben Hope so that only its northern flank, shouldering out onto the moor, was visible. Rain was coming. I climbed back down to the ridge, gathered my rucksack, and descended to the bealach, turning south and east towards the Flow Country.

Find the Ground

KARINE POLWART

The staccato bass of her accordion marks steady, unhurried time, whilst her right hand slinks across the keys in a stately maritime melody. Then, Inge sings:

> You stippled the sky
> A snowstorm of angels
> Deceiving my eye
> You've left me before
>
> Something's gone
> Something's lost
> Something's broken

It's a cool northerly flutter of a voice.

Composer, songwriter and multi-instrumentalist, Inge Thomson is my Midlothian neighbour, friend and band mate. But these are the opening bars and images of a song she wrote in minding of her childhood home, where much of her extended family lives amongst a total population of around sixty.

Fair Isle.

Three miles long, and one and a half miles wide, it rises halfway between Orkney's North Ronaldsay and the southern tip of Mainland Shetland.

We're listening to Inge's album *Da Fishing Hands*, and discussing it, as we sit at her kitchen table. She's conjuring a very different landscape to the one we live in here.

'On Fair Isle, you can always see the sea. You can always hear the sea. You can always taste the sea. Everything is immediate. The elements. The wind. Access on and off the Isle.'

She tells me that *The Good Shepherd IV* provides scheduled seaborne passage to and from Fair Isle once a week in winter, and up to three times a week in summer, wholly dependent on the weather. It's a two-and-a-half-hour somewhat stoic and unpredictable journey from Grutness Pier near Sumburgh to Fair Isle's North Haven. And the boat is aptly named for a lifeline service to a community whose wellbeing rests on a careful tending of shared resources. On the east side of the isle, the distinctive craggy promontory of Sheep Rock speaks to this. Until 1977, Fair Isle sheep were hauled up by rope from sea level to graze communally on its four hectares of precipitous summer pasture.

On the album, Inge continues to sing.

The shape of a glass
in the hands of the child,
shaken with sea spray

Here with feathers and facts
Mother Nature reacts
In the end we'll have no say

When the track ends, Inge explains. 'I was talking to Elizabeth Riddiford. Elizabeth said that when she first started coming to the isle, she would arrive on the plane, a wee eight-seater Islander at the north end of the isle, and there would be this massive flock of kittiwakes. She described it as like being in a snow globe, with "a snow-storm of angels" around you.'

After forty years on the isle, Elizabeth Riddiford is now embedded in its culture. She's a freelance knitter in the distinctive Fair Isle tradition that's still central to the island's economy, history and identity. She's also deeply knowledgeable about the flora and fauna of the island, notably the seabird colonies, for which the isle is also famed internationally.

So Elizabeth's poetic turn of phrase yielded Inge's song, 'The Snowstorm'. Part lament, part secular prayer, it was written for *Da Fishing Hands*, a song cycle album and performance project that Inge conceived with her cousin, esteemed Fair Isle poet and musician, Lise Sinclair.

In talking to islanders for research on *Da Fishing Hands*, Inge says that she and Lise heard the same story over and over, 'that the cliffs which had been white before with guano and white with birds, were now black, and a lot of them standing silent'.

Since 1948, Fair Isle Bird Observatory has built a global reputation as a scientific monitoring and research centre. Indeed, between 1981 and 1988, Elizabeth Riddiford's husband, ecologist Nick Riddiford, was Bird Obs Warden. Despite a devastating fire in March 2019, which destroyed the observatory building and forced the rehousing of current warden David Parnaby and his family, meticulous data collection on the isle continues.

Census records show a plummeting of kittiwake numbers in Fair Isle, from a 1988 high of 19,340 nesting pairs, to a low of 771 in 2013.

An island of eyes
With a careful gauge
For twenty years or more
We scrutinised the marks on the graph
The rise and fall of it all

Kittiwakes depend on a diet of sand eels, as do *Tammie Nories* (puffins), *tysties* (black guillemots) and *tirricks* (terns), all of which breed on Fair Isle too. When nearby sand eel stocks decline, adult birds are forced to feed far from their nests.

'I remember going out in the boat with my dad when I was about eleven or twelve,' recalls Inge, 'going around the west side of the island, and there being rafts of dead chicks, these little fluffy rafts of chicks, that had fallen off the cliffs. They'd starved. Their parents hadn't got back in time for feeding.'

The greatest threat to the sand eels on which kittiwakes depend was once industrial scale over-fishing in Shetland waters. Nowadays, warming seas and accelerating climate change disrupt the intertwined ecologies of phyto-plankton, which feed zooplankton, which feed sand eels, which feed the seabirds.

So what are we seeing here?
It's just the same snow globe
But the bubble's gone dry
We'll wait for the birds' response to the sky

Human industry and rising sea temperatures affect not only sand eels and seabirds, but the health of fish stocks all around Fair Isle, including *olicks* (ling), *piltocks* (coal fish) and *lye* (pollock).

The 'fishing hands' that lend their name to Inge and Lise's musical project are the historic fishing grounds of Fair Isle, known elsewhere in Shetland as *meads* or *grunds*. Usually they're identified by phrases based on two sets of fixed triangulation points, which enable fishermen to orientate themselves at sea. 'So, for example,' Inge reaches a pinched finger and thumb across the table, and draws an imagined line with her other hand, 'when a sea stack happened to line up with a landmark, and a hill with a line in the cliff, then you'd know you'd reached the grounds, you'd know where you were.' Both ancient rock formations and built human structures act as guides.

Like faces, seen from the sea
Rocks turn, familiar
Features fall into place

In Fair Isle, knowledge of where's best to fish has been passed between generations via a rich oral tradition, just as the island's knitting skills and traditional music have been passed hand-to-hand, and knee-to-knee. As Lise wrote in her lyric for the song 'Satellites', 'it takes a hundred years of days to know'.

When I first met Lise Sinclair, in 2003, she was singing a duet with her mother, singer and historian Anne Sinclair. I'd later stay with Anne on Fair Isle during Inge's wedding celebrations, and feed lambs at Lise's croft with my infant son. But our first connection was two thousand miles of ocean away at the annual Smithsonian Folklife Festival in Washington DC. There, in thirty-five-degree heat and 90 per cent humidity, Lise and Anne conjured the North Sea.

Starka virna vestilie
obadeea, obadeea
Starka virna vestilie
obadeea, monye

Strong blows the wind from the west
o trouble, trouble

Strong blows the wind from the west
o trouble, trouble for the men

A song not from Fair Isle, but from Unst, which is the northernmost of Shetland's islands, 'The Unst Boat Song' is Shetland's oldest surviving song fragment, in a mighty lineage of sea songs and lore. It's sung in Old Norn, an extinct language that leaves traces in modern Shetlandic, Norwegian and Icelandic.

Anne describes the song as 'a sea prayer, for the safe return of the men'. The men were, of course, fishermen, as they have always been in these waters.

'You know the old saying, Shetlanders are fishermen with crofts, and Orkney men are crofters with boats. In Shetland, the fishers are the heroes of the seas, the people all the songs were sung about,' says Inge.

'The Unst Boat Song' nods to millennia of fishing culture and economy in Shetland. And the oral knowledge of the fishing hands does too. But Inge says that since she was born in 1974, this means of orientation has become increasingly unreliable. Information about where to find fish was dying out because fishers could no longer be guaranteed a good catch, or any catch at all.

In 1995, prompted by concern around unstinting damage to the island's ecology, Nick Riddiford led the foundation of FIMETI, the Fair Isle Marine Environment and Tourism Initiative. It was from the outset a partnership between the Fair Isle Bird Observatory, the National Trust, which owns the island, and the Fair Isle community. A broad consideration of the environmental, economic and cultural value of Fair Isle's maritime ecology underpinned FIMETI's commitment to sustainability and collaboration 'for the benefit of the isle, its inhabitants, its visitors and the nation'. Crucially, FIMETI aimed 'to maintain and enhance the marine environment and related traditional activities currently and for future generations'.

It's hard to understand
why we need to take more,
more than a living,
more than can be held in store
emptying the sea like a river of gold
leaving nothing to the next generation at all

In 1999, under the auspices of FIMETI, Inge's sister-in-law, Emma Perring, published *Da Fishing Hands o' Fair Isle*, based on J. Eunson's 1961 collection *The Fair Isle Fishing Marks*. With the assistance of Inge's father, Stewart Thomson of Quoy, his cousin, Brian Wilson of Houll, and one of the oldest fishers on the isle, George Stout of Aesterhoull, Emma compiled an accompanying map, which is a striking visual representation of an ancient oral culture. Orientation points splinter out up to three miles from the ragged edges of Fair Isle in a geometric burst of intersecting shards. To a fisher, the names indicate how deep the seabed lies, whether it's sandy or hard bottomed, what kind of surface water conditions to expect and which fish you might find, in which season. The names have their own poetry:

*Da sooth end o'Buness by Sheep Rock and da eist end
o'Meoness seen through da inside o'da Burrian*

*Da Sooth Lighthoose a'tween da Twa Holms an da Kirk
seen through Roond Raiva*

To Inge, the map suggested itself immediately as a source
of graphic scores. And so the idea of the song cycle arose.
'We ended up with all these very spiky melodies,' she
says, diddling a fragment of 'East o'Buness' by way of
example. 'I drew round the coast of Fair Isle and then
imagined that the coastline was stretched onto a musical
stave as a melodic shape. A couple of melodies took parts
from that process. But if I'd done that with the whole
isle, it would have been torture!'

Fittingly, for a project that speaks to the entwined
ecologies of fish, seabirds and human habitation, it wasn't
only features of land and sea that offered melodic in-
spiration for *Da Fishing Hands*, but an improvised topography of Fair Isle speech too.

'Florrie Stout spoke very rhythmically,' Inge explains.
The late Florrie Stout was another isle knitter. Her
husband Jimmy was for many years the skipper of *The
Good Shepherd IV*, which Florrie herself formally launched
from its St Monans berth back in 1986. 'I got one of the
melodies from her speaking. I sat with the recording of
her voice and mapped how it was rising and falling onto
the page.' Florrie's cadence became an instrumental
passage in the song 'Satellites'. And in the instrumental
piece 'Dark Stacks', there's a snippet of Inge and Lise's

grandmother, Annie Thomson, reciting an old weather charm:

mackerel skies
and mare's tails
make tall ships
carry low sails

The voices of islanders were key to both the making of the 'fishing hands' map and to Inge and Lise's response to it. 'Lise coaxed out amazing gems from people's memories without it seeming like an interview,' says Inge. 'And I loved sitting down and speaking to some of the isle folk who don't necessarily have a voice, the folk that don't go to the meetings or have access to the Internet. We spoke to folk of all ages, older folks, the bairns, folks who'd come from overseas. It was important to get to folk that wouldn't write things down, or didn't have any sense of their own importance.'

Inge acknowledges that she and Lise had close connections to those they spoke with, and a shared understanding of people, place and culture. But she believes that artists have a potentially catalytic role to play in wider situations of human–animal conflict or environmental dispute.

'If you're making a piece of music about place, based on speaking to people, they have stories, they have their own emotional connections. It opens up a dialogue on something much deeper than you'd get at in a consultation meeting or on a form. There's a kind of trust that doesn't happen in courtrooms or boardrooms.'

In 2011, FIMETI submitted a proposal to the Scottish Government to designate Fair Isle a (Demonstration and Research) Marine Protected Area under the Marine (Scotland) Act 2010. The initial report, co-authored by Nick and Elizabeth Riddiford, was the first ever community-led campaign of its kind in Scotland. It had the unanimous support of Fair Isle residents.

Building trust was pivotal to FIMETI's campaign for MPA status. The question of fishing rights, in particular, revealed tensions between island communities across Shetland, as well as policy fault-lines at national and international level. There has been no commercial fishing in Fair Isle since the late 1950s, but fishing remains pivotal to other Shetland communities.

'What we didn't want to do with our writing is demonise the fishermen,' stresses Inge. 'That was already starting to happen in the media. Fishers were becoming public enemy number one.'

Securing support from the Shetland Fishing Federation for a five kilometre zone around Fair Isle designated for sustainable use marked a breakthrough point in FIMETI's lobbying for MPA status.

So we'll pray for the white rocks
and the silver's return to the sea

With our very last gasp
The air — is — still

But then, in April 2013, in the midst of writing for *Da Fishing Hands*, Lise Sinclair was diagnosed with brain cancer. After a short, ferocious illness, she died in August 2013, at the age of forty-two.

'An island's heart broke,' said Inge. She could scarcely imagine finishing the project that she and Lise had begun together, and offered to return all the funds.

However, in early autumn, not long after Lise's death, Inge was invited to join the crew of an old herring fifie called *The Swan*, which was sailing from Orkney to Mainland Shetland via Fair Isle. Its crew of maritime scientists and artists was sponsored by Cape Farewell, an international 'cultural response to climate change'.

I took part in the Orcadian leg of that trip. Indeed, I recall singing 'The Unst Boat Song' down below one evening in minding of Lise. As I stepped off *The Swan* in Stromness to head home, Inge joined for the Fair Isle crossing.

We share meat, we share light
We share wind and weather
Come aboard, come aboard
We'll do more together

Inge's telling me how she took the watch from one until four a.m. coming in towards Fair Isle, and shared the wheel of *The Swan* on approach. 'We held the boat off west for three hours the night before we came in. The swell was huge. We couldn't have got round the bottom of the isle. It's littered with wrecks. In those hours, I was just watching the light and holding, holding the boat off.'

The arrival of *The Swan* on the isle was an emotionally charged experience for Inge, the crew and the islanders who met them. She recalls a key conversation with Cape Farewell's Ruth Little. 'Ruth said, "You won't make the piece you started but you'll make the piece you need to make".'

The most important encouragement of all came from Anne Sinclair, Lise's mum. 'Her exact words were important and stuck with me. She said, "I don't just think you should do this, I think it's essential that you do." I left the isle feeling completely different about it.'

Inge immersed herself in the Fair Isle interviews she'd gathered with Lise, and throughout the writing process, Lise's voice was a constant presence in the recordings. Completing the final song of *Da Fishing Hands* was tough.

'"Song for Sheep Rock" was really hard for me to finish because Lise told me she had a tune for it, but I never heard it before she died. That song is about being lost, all out at sea, and then knowing where you are because of your environment, the landmarks, what's around you. The words were comforting. But knowing that she took the tune with her was very hard.'

This is a rock, salt truth,
a life and death story
to trust in every day.
As long as there's fish,
there's fish in the sea,

there's a heartbeat,
as long as there are fish in the sea.

On Fair Isle in May 2014, Inge and her band premiered *Da Fishing Hands* to a packed community hall.

In October 2016, Fair Isle became a Marine Protected Area, the first such designation awarded to a campaign led by local people. FIMETI has since made way for FIMRO, the Fair Isle Marine Research Organisation, which now manages the island environment on behalf of the entire community.

In Inge's kitchen, we listen to 'Song for Sheep Rock', the closing track of *Da Fishing Hands*. It ends with voices alone, in three-part a capella harmony. And with Lise's words –

I trace your features
til I know where I am,
find your face in my hands.
I'm learning to know you
every time we find the ground.

★ ★ ★

Lyrics used with permission are from 'The Snowstorm', 'Dark Stacks' and 'Wind and Weather' (words and music by Inge Thomson), from 'Song for Sheep Rock' and 'Satellites' (words by Lise Sinclair and music by Inge

Thomson) and from 'The Unst Boat Song' (traditional). *Da Fishing Hands* is available from ingethomson.com.

Sources:
Perring, Emma, *Da Fishing Hands o' Fair Isle*
Perring, Emma, *Fishing Traditions of Fair Isle* (The Orcadian Limited)

With thanks to Inge Thomson, Emma Perring, Nick Riddiford, Ian Best and Anne Sinclair.

The Bog-Eye of the Human

EM STRANG

LONICERA VULGARIS

Honeysuckle leaves have sprouted
and flourished along the side of a house.
So green, humans have to close their eyes
to imagine it, and even the long spring grass
is baffled. How to be a leaf
of such luminosity! How to sit so well
on a stem alongside others!

The leaves tenderly sway
in the slightest breeze, swaying, allowing,
as though their minds are made up
to affirm everything.

Here and there, humans
watch from small, rickety seats,
each barely visible to the other –
the grass is so tall.
The rooks easily outnumber them.

To learn such deep longing,
one must long for a long time.

ANTLERS OF WATER

THE MIRROR

If you're strong enough to hear it –
the blackbird has flown into the house!
It's a hot, airless day and the back door
was left wide for the bird. It's indisputable,
the dark blue door, its open width
and the matt black of the bird's coat,
his burnt wings and sun-ringed eye.

If you're strong enough to hear it –
the blackbird has flown upstairs!
He has followed the smell of water
and is listening to the streaming light
from his perch on the lip of the sink.
Here he meets his double, meets his double
and dances for the benefit of all blackbirds.

He is looking and seeing, hopping and waiting
for the other to disappear or die.

EM STRANG

THE BLAZING HOUSE

It's too quiet for the house to collapse
and burn bright red in the half-light.
A big wide mouth opens
and closes over the scene like a candle snuffer,
douses the flames
for ten seconds, maybe eleven.

Who is being born tonight into this?

THE FIELD

The field comes out at night
with its wide waiting and noiselessness.

Each furrow unravels itself
into the dark ocean of earth, the timeline
of everything hidden or hiding.

The field is never alone and knows
how kind the night is, to come so kindly
without fail, to sink down to its knees
unconditionally, to bring one field to another,
to bring the far burn invisibly to the river.

At dawn, hen pheasants slowly uncover
from hedgerows that no longer exist,
and the cock pheasants stand blazing
inside their own quiet fires,
like men who know how to love.

WATER OF AE

Don't wait to walk out along the back-roads
to the boggy fields where the swans are.
You can cross the river at the small bridge
and walk a walk you've walked for ten years
every day, even when the rain's on hard
and the wind's tearing at you. Don't wait
thinking you've seen it all already –
the flooded fields, the brown river,
the white swans. You can't see these things
from the bog-eye of the human. Don't wait.
Stride out with your boots on or, better still,
barefoot, and be inside the wind a while,
be inside the field like a grass halm might,
like a single blade awaiting sunlight.
Don't wait. Inevitably, it takes time
to unzip your hair, your skin, your face
enough to see swans, their blazing white,
but don't wait thinking you need better boots
or a waterproof that'll keep out the rain.
It won't. Don't wait. Walk out entirely
as though the mind is a rook's nest
in a tall, far-off Scots pine and behold
for the first time the swans, still there
after ten years of your looking, hunched
in the Scottish weather.
It doesn't matter how many similes
climb down from the rook's nest –
none of them fit. Don't wait.

From *A Place-Aware Dictionary*

ALEC FINLAY

ACCESS: the feeling of being allowed to walk or enter where one is allowed.

ANTHROPOCENE: us being too much for everything else.

ANTLER: a bone thorn; a stag's crown.
  '*The antlers are cast off in the spring and then begin to grow again. As they near their completion stags seek out mineral-rich earth to browse for nutrients. During the rut season stags enjoy thrashing a bush, or tree, in "mock combat", gathering broken branches and leaves to their antlers as decoration, and exaggerating their fearsome crown.*'
  (Rory Putman)

BEALACH: a way and the pass that leads through or over that way.
  Am Bealach Dearg, *The Reddy Way*
  Am Bealach Buidhe, *The Yellowy Way*

BEAT: a patch of moor set aside for driving deer or game.

BIT: a person's own place.
  '*Are you coming over to my bit to play?*' (Trad.)

BOG FIR: the roots of ancient pinewoods.
  Allt an Stuic Ghiubhais, *Bog-fir Burn*
  Am Branndair, *Tangled-root Bit*
  An Stocach, *Bog-fir Root-bit*
  Tom a' Bhranndair, *Tangled-root Knowe*
  Tom Fhreumhaigh, *Bog-fir Root-bit Knowe*

BOTHY: a rough dwelling for sharing, with a rapturous exterior attached.
  '*This bothy isn't fit for Sweeney, but have you seen the views?*' (Sandy Salmon)

BOWER: a woven dwelling for loving or healing.
  '*O Bessie Bell and Mary Gray / They war twa bonnie lasses / They biggit a bower on yon burn-brae / And theekit it o'er wi' rashes.*' (Trad. Ballad)

BURNING LAIRD: a laird addicted to grouse-moors and heather burning.
  'In a culture defined by burning carbon – peat or petrol – the term "burning laird" became a popular form of condemnation.' (*Scots Field*)

BUTT: hidey-hole for a gun.

CALEDONIAN PINEWOOD: the old native *fir-wood* which became *Native Pinewood*; which became *Caledonian Pinewood* to acknowledge the ancient boreal nature of woods descended from generation to generation by natural means, listed in *The Caledonian Pinewood Inventory*. This became the *Old Caledonian Pinewood* when the movement to plant from native seed created a *New Caledonian Pinewood* in the post-war era. These definitions reflect debates between restoring native woodland by planting and regenerating from existing pines.

   '*The native pine is a local genetic expression.*' (Jock Polmadie)

CALEDONIAN FOREST: an extent of woodland kept under peat.

CALLING: imitating a hind during the rut to lure a stag.
   '*The concept of luring a love-sick male by playing on his susceptibilities is repugnant to some people . . . Calling is perfectly legitimate, provided that it is used within the management plan, and not as a means of over-exploiting the deer population.*' (Richard Prior)

CAPERCAILLIE: a large performing bird, also known as *the great grouse*; from Gaelic *capall coille*, formerly *capercailzie, horse of the woods*; reintroduced in the eighteenth century, and very rare due to habitat loss and collisions with deer fences. Capercaillie are said to taste resinous.
   '*Male capercaillie . . . perform a complex display accompanied by a very unusual song. This initially starts with a*

gurgling sound accelerating to a drum roll followed by a popping sound and then finally a wheezing or gurgling sound to finish off, all of which is usually accompanied by a dance which ends in a "flutter jump".' (Lawrence Shove)

CHAIR (Gaelic, *cathaoir*): natural seat in the landscape; a prestigious viewpoint traditionally associated with royalty or saints, sometimes used for inauguration, as at Dùnadd and St Fillan's Chair, Dùndurn.

CHUM-YOU (Scots dialect): the offer of company on a short walk, usually along city streets.

'*We'll chum you doon the road.'* (Trad.)

COIHM-IMEACHD: from fairy-lore, referring to the other, twin, alter, or co-walker that each of us has (after Robert Kirk).

CONSPECTUS: a place to gaze at the landscape. Conspectuses are viewpoints where the terrain opens itself to the viewer; where the eye can thread in and out of the circle of hills; where place-names suggest a narrative sequence, offering the possibility of beginning to know where one is.

'*They spent the whole of that afternoon on the conspectus, learning the names and their meanings.'* (Chonzie Cockburn)

CONTEMPORARY TRANSHUMANCE: an umbrella term referring to the various activities that bring people back onto the hill – tree planting, humandwolving, and hutopianism. While this form of transhumance does not involve long-term dwelling in the uplands, in the sense of traditional shieling, it can benefit the hill ecologically.

CORRIE: a rough corner of the world; a kettled hollow in the hill.
  Lochan a' Choire Ghuirm, *Green Corrie Lochan*
  Coire Fhar, *Skyline Corrie*
  Coire na Ciche, *Tit Corrie*

COUNTERPANE: the imagination of blankets or bedding, and the form of a figure under them, as a rolling landscape, inspired by R.L. Stevenson's poem 'The Land of Counterpane'.

THE CRAZES: the Fingalian hunting cult which would define later Victorian and modern *crazes*, in particular, hunting and climbing; masculine fantasies and fashions which have dominated the Scottish wilderness.

CROWN: if human, a band of gold, similar to an antler; if pine then republican.

DAUNER, DAUNDER: a Scottish version of the walk that drifts. *Daun'rin' Kate* is a byname for stonecrop.

DAY OF ACCESS: an annual day when the walking constrained and disabled are conveyed in vehicles using estate roads to restore their rightful experience of hills and wild nature. The first Day of Access was held near Schiehallion in June 2019.

EARTH OTHER: term coined by Val Plumwood to refer to the more than human, i.e. all of the beings that populate the earth's biotic community.

'In terms of Earth Law and questions of the rights of Earth Others, how might food be produced if the plants, animals, soils, and waters on which we depend each had their own right to health?' (Becca S. Tarnas)

ECOSYSTEM: a collection of names, insects and worms.

'Rooting wild boar are wonderful ecosystem engineers due to their impact on vegetation.' (Daisy Lingonberry)

'We are all ecosystems: the difference is, people are aware of their relative health or illness, while ecologies have no idea whether they are sick or well.' (Donna Farraway)

EILEIRIG (Gaelic): a natural deer-trap formed between two hills into which deer were driven for slaughter.

'The great meet place, to which all the deer were driven to was at the Hill of Elrick, on Dirnanean Moor which hill, as its name indicates, had been for ages one of the noted hunting places of Athole . . . This enclosure was always overlooked by an overhanging rock or hill called Craggan-an-Elrick, from which ladies could see the sport in safety.' (Charles Ferguson)

ESTATE: a vast tract of untended land set aside for the use of visitors in August.

ESTATE ROAD: a track into the hills to allow people who can walk to drive.

FIANNSCAPE: the mytho-poetic ballads of the Fingalians were projected imaginatively on topography, using totemic place-names to create a poetic landscape, or Fiannscape; the most famous examples of these early works of Land Art are in Glenshee and Glenelg.

FIELD-RECORDING: a landscape or seascape portrayed using an outdoor microphone.
  '*Field-recordings are the concertos of place-awareness.*' (Alec Finlay)

FIRE: an improving disaster; burning heather for grouse moors, or to clear an understorey for seedlings to thrive in pinewoods.

FOLKLORE: a supernatural glow that diminishes from generation to generation.

FOLLY: a whim of fashion built in stone; a craze for Fingalian follies and tree-plantings focused on Perthshire.
  '*That year my nephew gave me a folly for my birthday.*' (James, 2nd Duke of Atholl)

FORAGER: an expert in the menu of the hedgerow; one who enjoys jarring, mushrooming, berrytime and scrumping. Later sometimes referred to as the Brexit Diet.

'*Many things can be foraged, some only once.*' (Trad.)

FOREST: a hill terrain translated into a hunting territory by means of exchanging trees for deer; later used by Forestry Commission Scotland as a designation for a plantation.

'*One forest forms one unit / And all parts are the same, / No matter where located, / They must bear the unit name!*' (From 'The Forest of Strathnairn: The Wayfarer and the Commissioner' by Murdo MacAskill)

FORESTER: one who stalks deer.

FOG HOUSE: an octagonal hut with heather-thatch that gathers moss (Scots. fog), designed for thinking into and looking out of.

FORESTRY COMMISSION: the recruitment office for forestry plantations.

GREEN LAIRD: a laird dedicated to tree planting and landscape remediation.

GRIANÁN: sun-bower; a sunny chamber, bender, shieling or soller; a summer dwelling in a sunny spot, most famously Deirdre's Tigh Grianan in Glen Etive, a fantasy of transhumance, like Deirdre and her '*fauld o' sunbeams*', to quote Hugh MacDiarmid.

HORIZON: a rest for the eyes; a day's walk.

HUMAN: an animal with maps.

HUMANDWOLF: the practice of filling the niche of the wolf as a means to ward deer from saplings; Project Wolf was devised by Doug Gilbert in 2016 and trialled at Trees for Life Dundreggan.
   '*When I'm out there being a humandwolf I want for nothing, except maybe dry socks, but when I'm back home I want more than anything to go back.*' (Anon. humand-wolf)

HUNTING: a form of conservation based on killing.
   '*There is more to hunting than killing; there is more to stalking than shooting.*' (Sandy Salmon)

HUTOPIANISM: the contemporary innovative renewal of huts and bothies, encouraging dwelling in wild nature and mountain culture. Hutopianism allows people to dwell in juniper woods, heather moors and the upper glens, reviving the imagination of what it means for these places to be lived in and cared for.
   '*They had that wild poetic manner of hutopians.*' (Sweeney Niven)

LEK: from Swedish *leka*, a rite of foreplay; a cock fight dance performed by capercaillie or black-cock, featuring a flutter jump. Black-cock calls include *rrooo-oo-rroo-rroo, tshooo-whch,* and *koo-ke-rroo.*

MADADH, MHAIDIDH (Gaelic): confusingly this refers to the wolf and the dog; also in Gaelic we find *madadh-ruadh*, fox, and *madadh-donn*, otter.

MAP: a memory of landscape or an illustrated poem.
  '*Watch where you're going; the artist is reading the map.*'
  (Padraig Eyres)

MARGINAL GARDEN: part of the wilds set aside from the wilderness; the leading theorist of the marginal garden movement was the molecular biochemist, poet, and climber G.F. Dutton, who created a notable garden near Bridge of Cally.
  '*Marginal gardeners are shepherds of plants – encourage them here or there, comfort them in a crisis, but never drive your flora.*' (A.F. after G.F. Dutton)

MUIRBURN: flags of fire; burning heather on grouse-moors, one of the most intensive human interventions in land management in northern Europe.
  '*Under the old shieling system, when the cattle plus a few sheep, goats and ponies all went up to the hill grazings in May or June and stayed there until the crops downbye had been harvested in September, there would have been little need for muirburn.*' (Reay D.G. Clarke)

NICHE: an ecological locale identified with a specific flora or fauna; the human *bit* overlaps with the animal *niche*.
  Clais nan Cat, *Wildcat's Niche*

PARK: an expanse of landscape where city people store their better natures; a large patch of landscape in which humans wander through the habitats of earth others.
  '*Instead of scattered huts, lynx and pinewoods, the park had a funicular.*' (Cameron McIlhose)

PATH: a following held in common.
  '*Trust a deer path over a human path.*' (Frank Fraser Darling)

PINE-PLANTING TRIBE: contemporary social movement dedicated to reforestation and rewilding.
  '*She had dreads and smelt of peat, like one of the pine-planting tribe.*' (J.K. Tolling)

PIP: acronym of Pearls in Peril; small exclosures of native broadleaves planted for the benefit of fresh-water pearl mussels and salmon.
  '*PIP plots are a model of the great wood.*' (Jock Polmadie)

PLACE-AWARENESS: the experience of place informed by culture and lore, especially the meanings of place-names and their relationship to ecology.

PLACE-NAME: a name used to identify a field of biotic relationships, or an act of imaginative possession.
  Meall nan Eun, *Lambs Knowe*
  Allt a' Mhadaidh, *Wolf Burn*
  Caochan Bheithe, *Birch Burnie*

POEM-LABEL: a tag for a haiku or short poem to tie to grasses or branches; in Japanese, *tanzaku*.

> '*He scattered his poem-labels out on the floor like he was casting an I-Ching.*' (Alasdair Thurso)

PROXY WALK: a walk done on behalf of a person who is bed-/house-bound with illness, describing the present reality of a landscape they recall; an act of imaginative solidarity and exchange of energy.

RAPTOR: a bird that feeds on prey and dies on grouse moors.

> '*The old keepers thought any raptor with a hooked beak was to be eliminated.*' (Lea MacNally)

REWILDING: restoring a niche of land to its uncultivated state and allowing natural processes to interact without human intervention; the reintroduction of totemic native species into a locale as an act of fidelity to nature, or the imaginative recreation of an ecology for ethical reasons.

RUT: the warring of horny stags competing for a harem of hinds; September 20th is the traditional start of the rut.

> '*The master stag entered, peat-blackened, hoary-muzzled, thick-chested, high-headed, wide-antlered, barrel-necked, and, with the wind working mercifully in my favour, he stank.*' (Jim Crumley)

SANCTUARY: an area of deer forest that is pacifist.
'*Stags have been observed feeding within sanctuary when stalking or grouse-shooting was going on just outside the sacred precincts.*' (Alexander Inkson McConnochie)

SHIELING: the local commons of the hill; the summer-town.
Auchiries, *Shieling-bit*
Knock na Hare, *Shieling Hill*
Sealscrook, *Shieling Knock*
Fuaran Ruighe an Fhraoich, *Heather-shiel Well*

SHOOT: if a bullet, to wound; if a plant, a sucker or new growth.

SÌTHEAN, SÌDHEAN: a drumlin mistaken for a fairy-knowe, raised by no natural power, giving entrance to another world; a fairy hillock, for *Subterranean Cavern-inhabitants* (Kirk), typically found near a shieling.
'*There Be manie places called Fayrie hills, which the mountain-people think impious and dangerous to peel or discover, by taking earth or wood from them . . .*' (Robert Kirk)
Ben Hee, *Fairy Ben*
Sìdhean an Airgid, *Silver Fairy-knowe*
Cnoc nan Sìthean, *Fairy-knock*

SOFTS: to walk on bare feet.
'*Fraser-Darling followed the deer-herd in his softs.*' (Robbie McFurling)

STEWARDSHIP: a progressive and ecologically focused corrective to conventional estate management, nurturing biodiversity and traditional skill; the term was popularised by the Falkland Centre for Stewardship.

STORM: a means of strengthening woods.

STRAVAIG: a walk seasoned with Scots.
  'Why, oh why must these Scottish novelists go on about stravaiging whenever they go for a walk?' (Jane Houston)

SUMMERTOWN: shieling in the uplands traditionally used from May to autumn; a place of sharing learning, lore and sleeping on heather and myrtle; the farm-town where people lived for the rest of the year was known as *the wintertown*.

SUIDHE (Gaelic): seat; a prominence set aside for sitting and looking; a seat of power. *Suidhe* were traditionally associated with viewing the hunt; they overlooked an *eilrig*, deer-trap. They are also associated with saints, suggesting the power of the Celtic Church, or with royal investiture. (See above: chair, cathaoir).
  Suidhe Finn, *Fionn's Seat*
  St Fillan's Seat
  King's Seat

TAINCHELL (Gaelic): deer drive, from Gaelic, *tàin*, herd, describing the tradition of driving deer into a narrow corrie, or eileirig, for slaughter. The last such hunt was held by the Duke of Sutherland, to honour a visit from King Alfonso of Spain in 1928.

'. . . because the deir will be callit upwart ay be the tainchell, or without tynchell they will pass upwart perforce.'
(Sir Donald Monro)

TERRITORY: a measure of energy (animal), or arena of power (human).

'One cause of black-cock mortality in spring from year three and onwards was associated with intense territorial display.' (Per Angelstam)

VSW (VERY SHORT WALK): a walk that measures up for the chronically ill, also known as a Minor Walk.

'His favourite minor walk was from the roadside to MacBeth's Hillock, where he liked to picnic.' (Fooley's *Life of Chnozie*)

VIEW: as far as the moment sees.

WALK: as far as the day goes.

WALKING-CONSTRAINED: those who cannot walk far due to chronic illness.

WILD GARDEN: a garden for overlooking.

★ ★ ★

With thanks to Marlene Creates for terms relating to walking from the Dictionary of Newfoundland English; *Tim Collins and Gordon Eaglesham for discussion on the definitions of rewilding; Ken Cockburn for our collaboration on* Johnson's Dictionary: A Supplement, Out of Books. *Some of these definitions refer to earlier projects such as* the road north *and* The Perthshire Folly Tour *(both with Ken Cockburn) and* gathering.

the-road-north.blogspot.com
out-of-books.com
follytour.blogspot.com

Swimming Away from My Baby

AMY LIPTROT

When I first started swimming with the Orkney Polar Bears, women in the club with young children told me that they swam in the sea because it was the only place where their kids wouldn't follow them. It's only now, several years later and with a toddler of my own, that I realise they weren't joking.

The winter before I was pregnant, I swam outdoors once a week. I was fit and cold adapted. But pregnancy brought nausea and exhaustion. I grew softer and slower but was determined to stay active and get outdoors. Mainly I stuck to gentle walks but there were a few memorable swims that summer. I remember swimming in the hilltop reservoir soon after the scan which told me I was carrying a boy. He became clearer in my mind and I smiled to myself as I swam out into the water which rippled like silk. I was not alone; I had my son with me.

As well as the reservoir, I swam in rivers, lakes, the sea and in indoor pools. I lounged in hot baths. I even had a couple of sessions in a flotation tank. As my baby floated in his pool of amniotic fluid, I floated in my tank of highly salted water, bloated and buoyant, the weight taken off my limbs and joints for a delicious hour, my mind drifting free.

Sometimes I didn't swim. At five months pregnant, I joined the Orkney Polar Bears at Tingwall jetty but it just didn't feel right and I watched from the pier-side with the herring gulls, wrapped in my warm jacket. At seven months pregnant, in October, I swam under a waterfall in chilly water flowing down from the hills. After a couple of minutes, my belly tightened alarmingly and I got out immediately. It was to be my last swim before I became a mother.

Cold-water swimming offered me some preparation for giving birth. Swimming through winter taught me that I was stronger than I thought, so I could face labour, something so many have been through. Entering cold water had shown me that there is some subjectivity to pain. When I first swam in the sea, the cold felt painful, like burning, and I would sharply inhale and yelp as I entered. But with time, I learned that exhaling as I took the plunge made it easier, relaxing into the water. I could experience the cold as 'strong sensation' rather than pain. And, swimming regularly, I knew that if I passed that threshold I could survive and even enjoy it. I took these lessons with me into childbirth.

On Christmas Eve, I laboured all night in a birth pool. The warm water held me for those hours as I entered a new, deep, solitary place of mental strength. I could not stop the excruciating contractions coming but instead tried to ready myself for each one, not to fight it, the way I'd learned to work with waves at the Bay of Skaill.

Ten weeks after giving birth, snow was on the ground but, spurred on by a brave friend, I was back in the water again. We swam for seconds rather than minutes but I was jubilant. I was back and it felt like a real milestone. In the water it was wonderful to move my body freely. I appreciated it more than ever.

In the early months of motherhood, time to swim had to be carefully planned and executed. I'd set my alarm for sunrise so I could be home again in a couple of hours, just as the baby needed another feed. On the way home, my pulse would quicken. When I got home I'd feel like I'd pulled off a magic trick, like I'd dreamed my swim. The salt in my hair was proof that the world still existed outside my baby bubble of blankets and milk.

On the spring equinox I fed the baby at 5.15 a.m. then left him in bed with his dad. I put on my warmest layers and drove out of town. I parked and after a short climb was up at the hilltop reservoir just as the sun rose. A kestrel hovered. There were patches of snow. Unusually, there was barely any wind at the top and the water was glassy, reflecting the sunrise, icy around the shallowest edges. I took some photographs, then stripped and waded in. It was perhaps the coldest water I'd ever been in but I barely hesitated. *I've given birth; I am indestructible.* I only swam for twenty or so strokes, swearing, shocked into fear by the temperature. On the walk back down I saw ravens, wild geese and lapwings in courtship dance. Despite the cold, it was almost spring.

It takes more planning to arrange outdoor swimming when someone else needs to hold the baby. But every time I managed it, I thought *I should do this more often.* The seasons progressed, it got milder, and the baby and his dad watched from the bank as I swam with my friend. My friend rescued a bee from the water and swam with it in his raised hand back to shore. Afterwards in the pub, I ate ravenously. *Swimming gives me a good appetite. Breastfeeding gives me a good appetite.*

And while swimming, I felt relieved. Although the baby was not far away, he was with someone else and I briefly let myself abandon responsibility for him in my mind and, realising my relief, cried a little. For five months now I was always thinking of him, a large strand of my awareness with him. I was constantly stretched a little tightly.

Gradually, I could spend longer away from him – a whole morning, a whole day. I had a gorgeous almost-even-warm swim up at the reservoir. There were larks, stonechats and swallows, catching insects on the water at my eye level.

In the spring, we dipped his feet in the sea for the first time. The summer was hot and we walked up to the reservoir often, taking turns to go for a dip while the other held the baby. The water was warm and glorious and I stayed in for longer, under swallow screams and skylark song.

My best friend, who had a baby ten days before me,

came to stay. On midsummer evening, after the babies were asleep, we jumped in my car and went for a swim in the river. We played loud music. I smoked two cigarettes. I wore no clothes.

It was hot for weeks: a heatwave. The grass grew parched and the water warm. Sometimes in the evening, I ran away from my family to swim. I ran away with myself. The reservoir was deep blue and warm in pockets. I did backstroke and looked at the open sky.

When the baby was seven months old, we took a van trip up the north-west coast of Scotland. We spent nights beside the sea and lochs and I swam where I could. I had a thrilling sea swim where a flock of waders (sanderling? dunlin?) gave me a fly-past at water level. There were small moon jellyfish and two grey seals.

At Kinlochewe, I saw a buzzard while I was swimming. The seaweed felt silky on my skin. My bacon and eggs tasted great afterwards. I worried slightly that anyone who saw me wading into the Scottish sea that misty morning might think I was killing myself when in fact it was the opposite: I was aliving myself.

My baby can become a bit alarmed as, my partner or mum holding him on the beach or beside the loch, he watches me wade into the water. Psychoanalyst Donald Winnicott wrote about the stage of early child development where the baby comes to realise that its mother is a separate entity. I am going somewhere he cannot follow and the baby realises he is not omnipotent. I feel my heart tugging, part of it left behind on the beach, but I want to swim and I think it is good for both of us. I may walk into the sea but the important thing, of course, is that I always come back.

I am more cautious than I used to be. In Orkney, I don't swim out to the rusting old shipwreck with some of the stronger swimmers in the club, but hang back by the shore, hearing their laughter and watching arctic terns.

Later in the trip, we met and swam after dark at Scapa Bay, hearing seals howl and watching the lights of oil tankers out to sea. I managed a few minutes in the darkly rippling water, seaweed on my legs, stars coming out above. Afterwards I was flushed with pride: I survived! The survival is what makes it feel so good and I returned to my warm sleeping family.

At midwinter, I plunged into a mill pond for around forty-five seconds. The water was about five degrees. Hours later, after food and a bath, my skin and mind still felt more alive than usual. My baby turned one on Christmas Day.

I went alone with my son for a seaside holiday in January, avoiding the builders at home. I did not swim; it would have been impossible. Swimming in the sea is not compatible with being in sole care of a baby. I require assistance and am more vulnerable than before. I have never lost my respect for the sea.

I've swum less since I've been a mother but the swims have meant more. I manage it maybe a couple of times a month. I've swum with other mothers of young children whom I've met in the last two years. It feels like a silly, funny thing to do; we become the childish ones. I take notes:

It was raining when we swam today / a big old heron / soil scent & grey haze / nature's steam room

this morning I swam with a rainbow and swallows. Ridiculous!

My sobriety anniversary. Celebrated, as ever, with a screamingly cold swim. Skylarks going bonkers, a little sun.

Mother's Day swim with skylarks and geographers.

Magical solstice nightswim under Jupiter, bats and noctilucent (nightshining) cloud!

High summer swim at the reservoir, in balmy water under dreamy sky.

I was all wound-up and nervy this morning but got up to the reservoir for a swim this afternoon and it's sorted me right out.

Got up early / Climbed a hill / And swam inside a cloud.

About the Authors

Jacqueline Bain is a former nurse and support worker with Alzheimer Scotland. Her writing on immobility and its impact on her relationship with nature was shortlisted for the Nan Shepherd Prize in 2019. She has had nature pieces published in *Mslexia* and the *Summer* and *Winter* editions of *An Anthology for the Changing Seasons*, edited by Melissa Harrison, as well as short stories in the *People's Friend*, *Take-A-Break Fiction-Feast* and *Writing Magazine*. She lives in Paisley.

Anne Campbell studied painting at Edinburgh College of Art before returning to live in her native village of Bragar, on the west side of Lewis. She has studied the island environment through the disciplines of art, archaeology and natural history, exploring the interaction between the land and the living things which spend their lives here or pass through: the traces left behind, whether on the earth and stones or in the memory and imagination.

annecampbellart.co.uk

Jim Carruth's first collection, *Bovine Pastoral*, came out in 2004 and has been followed by seven further chapbooks and three book-length collections. His poetry has been shortlisted for the Saltire Scottish Poetry Book of the Year Award, the Seamus Heaney Centre For Poetry Prize and the Fenton Aldeburgh Prize for first collection. He is the current Poet Laureate of Glasgow and his most recent collection, *Bale Fire*, came out in 2019.

jimcarruth.co.uk

Linda Cracknell is a writer of fiction, non-fiction and drama for whom landscape, place and memory are key themes. She has published two collections of short stories, a novel – *Call of the Undertow* (2013) involving maps and a character in exile in coastal Caithness – and *Doubling Back: Ten Paths Trodden in Memory* (2014), an account of a series of walks, each of which follow a story from the past. Linda lives in Highland Perthshire.

@LindaJCracknell | lindacracknell.com

Jim Crumley has been a full-time Scottish nature writer for more than thirty years, and is the author of forty books. He has been shortlisted for a Saltire Society Book Award, the Wainwright Prize, the Boardman-Tasker Prize for Mountain Literature and the Banff International Mountain Book Award in Canada. His most recent work is a tetralogy based on the seasons; the final volume, *The Nature of Summer*, was published in June 2020.

ABOUT THE AUTHORS

Alec Finlay is an artist and poet whose work crosses over a range of media and forms. He established morning star publications in 1990. He has published over forty books and won seven Scottish Design Awards, including two Grand Prix Awards. Recent publications include: *A Far-off land* (2018); *gathering* (2018); *th' fleety wud* (2017), *minnmouth* (2017) and *A Variety of Cultures* (2016).

alecfinlay.com

Gavin Francis is a GP and the author of *Adventures in Human Being*, which won the Saltire Scottish Non-Fiction Book of the Year Award, *Empire Antarctica*, which won Scottish Book of the Year in the SMIT Awards and was shortlisted for both the Ondaatje and Costa Prizes, and most recently *Island Dreams*. He has written for the *Guardian*, *The Times*, the *New York Review of Books* and the *London Review of Books*. His books are translated into eighteen languages. He lives in Edinburgh.

@gavinfranc | gavinfrancis.com

David James Grinly is an artist from Alva. His work regards the intersections of thought, image and belief via the photographic. He lectures in critical studies, and works as a Research Associate in a gallery in Edinburgh.

davidjamesgrinly.com
instagram.com/davidjamesgrinly

Jen Hadfield is a poet published by Picador, whose fourth collection *The Stone Age* (Picador, 2021) explores neuro-diversity. She is also working on a collection of essays about Shetland, where she is building a house very slowly.
  @hadfield_jen

Lesley Harrison lives and works on the Angus coastline. Her poetry and prose draw from archive, folk myth and cultural memory to make real the sense of living at the temperate edge of a much older sub-polar world. She has held writing residencies in Iceland, Svalbard and Greenland. Her most recent collections are *Blue Pearl* (New Directions) and *Disappearance* (Shearsman).
  lesleyharrisonpoetry.wordpress.com

Sally Huband lives in Shetland and received a Scottish Book Trust New Writers Award in Narrative Non-Fiction in 2017.

Amy Liptrot is the *Sunday Times* bestselling author of *The Outrun*, which was awarded the Wainwright Prize and the PEN Ackerley Prize, and was shortlisted for the Wellcome Prize and the Ondaatje Prize. As well as writing for newspapers including the *Guardian* and the *Observer*, Amy has worked as an artist's model, a trampolinist and in a shellfish factory.
  @amy_may

Gerry Loose is a poet living on the Isle of Bute who works with subjects from the natural world, as well as the world of geopolitics. His work can be found inscribed and created in parks, botanic gardens, natural landscapes, in galleries and on the page. His awards include a Robert Louis Stevenson Fellowship, Creative Scotland Award, Kone Foundation Award and a Hermann Kesten Fellowship. His most recent book is *The Great Book of the Woods* (Xylem Books, 2020).

gerryloose.com

Hayden Lorimer writes about past places and living landscapes, in Scotland and elsewhere. He is a Professor of Human Geography in the School of Geosciences at the University of Edinburgh.

@Slipshodspeller

Garry MacKenzie is a poet and non-fiction writer based in Fife. His poetry has been published in journals including *The Clearing*, *The Compass Magazine* and *Dark Mountain*. He was awarded a residency at Cove Park in 2019, is a recipient of a Scottish Book Trust New Writers Award and won the Wigtown Poetry Competition in 2016. His book *Scotland: A Literary Guide for Travellers* was published by I.B. Tauris. He teaches creative writing and literature.

garrymackenzie.com.

Karine Polwart is a songwriter, musician, theatre-maker, and writer. Her solo theatre work *Wind Resistance* (with the Royal Lyceum Theatre), weaves together peatland ecology, goose flight, folklore and midwifery (text published by Faber). She is a 2020 Artist in Residence at the Royal

Botanic Garden Edinburgh. And she's currently thinking and writing about village greens, nuclear time and ginger.

@IAMKP | karinepolwart.com

Chris Powici's writing explores the ways that human life and wildlife rub up against each other. His latest collection of poems, *This Weight of Light*, is published by Red Squirrel. He edited the literary magazine *Northwords Now* from 2010 to 2017 and teaches creative writing for the University of Stirling and The Open University. Chris lives in Perthshire, whose roads and tracks, as well as those of other counties, he loves to cycle.

Chitra Ramaswamy is an award-winning author and journalist. Her first book, *Expecting: The Inner Life of Pregnancy*, was published by Saraband in 2016. It won the Saltire First Book of the Year Award and was shortlisted for the Polari Prize. She is from London and lives in Leith, Edinburgh, with her partner, two young children and rescue dog.

@Chitgrrl

Jess Smith is an author and storyteller. From her child-hood memories of travelling the old roads of Scotland with a devoted family in a Bedford bus, she wrote her classical trilogy of *Jessie's Journey* books. She has shared her cultural stories and songs at many international book and storytelling festivals, and also works in prison libraries, schools and hospitals.

jesssmith.co.uk

Dougie Strang is a writer and performer. He lives with his wife and two daughters by the River Ae in south-west Scotland and is currently writing a book about landscape and folklore.

@DougieStrang | dougiestrang.org

Em Strang is a poet, novelist and founder of Scottish charity Three Streams, facilitating resilience, wellbeing and creative freedom at a time of global crisis. Her first full collection, *Bird-Woman*, was published by Shearsman in 2016, was shortlisted for the Seamus Heaney Best First Collection Prize and won the 2017 Saltire Poetry Book of the Year Award. Her second collection, *Horse-Man*, was published in 2019. Her first novella, *Quinn*, was shortlisted for the 2019 Fitzcarraldo Editions Novel Prize.

em-strang.co.uk

Malachy Tallack is an award-winning author and singer-songwriter. His most recent book, *The Valley at the Centre of the World* (2018), was published by Canongate. It was shortlisted for the Highland Book Prize and longlisted for the Royal Society of Literature Ondaatje Prize. His previous books are *Sixty Degrees North* (2015) and *The Un-Discovered Islands* (2016). Malachy is from Shetland, and currently lives in Dunblane.

@malachytallack | malachytallack.com

Amanda Thomson is a visual artist and writer who lives and works in Glasgow and Strathspey. A lot of her work – in art and writing – is about the Highlands of Scotland, its landscape and nature, and how we are located (and locate ourselves) in the world. Her first book, *A Scots Dictionary of Nature*, was published by Saraband Books in 2018.

@passingplace | passingplace.com

Introduced by **Robert Macfarlane**   Afterword by **Jeanette Winterson**

THE LIVING MOUNTAIN
NAN SHEPHERD

'The finest book ever written on nature
and landscape in Britain'
GUARDIAN

'A masterpiece of Scottish nature writing'
Observer

CANON▮▮GATE

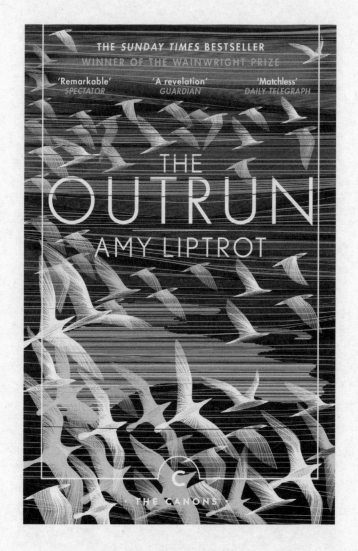

THE *SUNDAY TIMES* BESTSELLER
WINNER OF THE WAINWRIGHT PRIZE

'Remarkable'
SPECTATOR

'A revelation'
GUARDIAN

'Matchless'
DAILY TELEGRAPH

THE OUTRUN

AMY LIPTROT

THE CANONS

'A luminous, life-affirming book'
Olivia Laing

CANON❙❙GATE

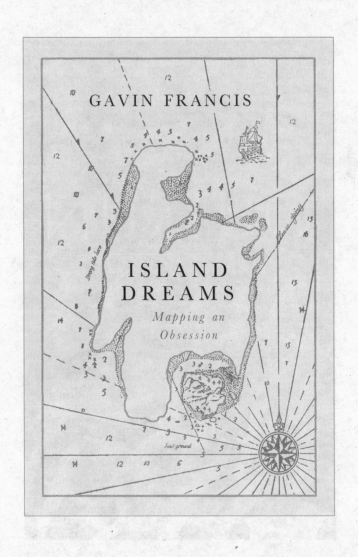

GAVIN FRANCIS

ISLAND
DREAMS

*Mapping an
Obsession*

'A thrilling book – beautiful and spare'
Tim Dee

CANON❙❙GATE